Adventure in Understanding

Adventure in Understanding

Talks to Parents, Teachers and Librarians

by

Lois Lenski

1944 - 1966

with decorations by
the author

Published by

The Friends of the Florida State University Library
Tallahassee, Florida
1968

CONTENTS

POEMS

ACKNOWLEDGMENTS

All poems except four are from THE LIFE I LIVE: Collected Poems, Henry Z. Walck, Inc. 1965; used by permission of the author.

"Living," "Git sand in Your Shoes," "Out in the Piney Woods," and "Dear Child" copyright 1968 by Lois Lenski.

"Seeing Others as Ourselves" *The Horn Book Magazine,* v. 22, no. 6, July-Aug., 1946. Used by permission.

"Regional Children's Literature" *Wilson Library Bulletin,* v. 21, no. 4; Dec., 1946. Used by permission.

"Getting Books from Life." *Kent State University Bulletin,* v. 43, no. 12; Dec. 1955. Used by permission.

"Creating Books" *School Library Journal,* v. 10, no. 2; Oct. 1963. Used by permission.

"Place and People" *Illinois State University Journal,* v. 28, no. 3. Feb. 1966. Used by permission.

"A Story from Strangers" (former title: "How Do I Do It?") *Lois Lenski Collection,* Florida State University, 1966. Used by permission.

Preface

GROWING UP *in a home where books are read is a wondrous thing. Greater still is the pleasure of reading to one's children and grandchildren. Among the most popular books in our household for this type of reading, and the favorites of the children, grandchildren, parents and grandparents alike are the Lois Lenski books. The most favorite of all, of course, is our copy of* The Little Family *with the inscription in her mother's handwriting to our first child, Barbara, on her second birthday. This little volume was not only Barbara's favorite book during this period of her life but 25 years later it was the favorite book of her daughter, Wendy, as well.*

This first little book which introduces the child to Lois Lenski will lead him to the other Lois Lenski books as he grows and matures.

Something just a little more expressive seemed always to brighten up the faces of these two little girls as we enjoyed together the Lois Lenski books. The sparkle in their eyes seemed just a little brighter, and there was just a little more eagerness in the anticipation of the well known line and of the illustration on the next page. The cause of this I never really tried to discover and I always just let it go at, "They are Lois Lenski books."

Years later when I became personally acquainted with Miss Lenski and had the opportunity to hear her speak and the privilege of visiting in her home I began to be more aware of her philosophy of life and her way of writing and creating books. Then it became quite clear to me why her books always contained that something extra that appeals to young people.

Recently I asked Miss Lenski if she would get together a collection of her talks. This volume is a result of my inquiry and it brings together in book form many of her ideas concerning books and literature in general, young people, our world and particularly her own ideas on writing and the creation of books for children. Included also are a number of her poems.

N. Orwin Rush
Tallahassee, Florida
January 1968

Foreword

Wonderful World

WHAT DOES *my work mean to me?*

Making books for children is, of course, always sheer enjoyment. I am often asked why I do not write for adults. With all due respect to the fine adult authors whose works I know and love, I say frankly: I would not change places with them for the world!

I think the greatest satisfaction in work for children comes from the knowledge that such work is constructive, building up, building for the future. We feel this poignantly in war-time, in these days of the terrible destruction of physical things and of spiritual values. We want to lead our children wisely, to help them develop as individuals to live together harmoniously in spite of differences of opinion. We want to help them to think clearly as never before and to avoid the mistakes we have made.

But work for children is not so much leading, influencing, directing; it is not even, primarily, giving! *It is usually just* taking! *Yes, because always we get back so much in return for the little we give.*

What a wonderful world it is, if we are fortunate enough to find the key to open the door—this world where children live! It is a world where there is always joy, beauty and hope; where sorrows are short-lived or non-existent; where there is constant faith, trust and respect for all, even for undeserving adults; where nothing that has *happened or* can *happen will mar the joy of living.*

To share that life, to understand their point of view, to become a child with them, with their clearness of vision, their keenness of imagination and their spontaneous enjoyment of beauty, surely no one could ask for a greater privilege than that. Only by taking from them and constantly en-

riching our own lives, can we possibly hope to help them.

Perhaps we are idealists, we authors of children's books. At any rate, we never for a moment believe that children really like the cheap, the tawdry and the commonplace. If that is what they feed on, it is because they have been given nothing better. We know, that once they are given the opportunity, they will always respond. As instinctively as flowers turn toward the sunshine, they will respond to the good, the true and the beautiful, and so we try to give it to them.

In the writing and illustrating of my many books, I have been not so much the creator as an instrument, a go-between, an interpreter. I like to feel that by telling old truths again in a new dress, these truths may become more readily acceptable to children in the present age. In the writing of my books I have felt a compelling urge to say certain things that have been put into my heart to say, and to say them honestly and openly. In breaking down a few taboos in the field of children's literature, perhaps we move forward to a better understanding of children and their needs.

Through my books I have tried to do a num-

ber of things for children. I have tried to give them the enjoyment of good stories easy to read, illustrated so richly that the illustrations tell the story as well as the text. I have hoped also that while getting pleasure out of the reading, children may also learn some new ideas and acquire new insights. In other words, I have hoped that my books will inspire thoughtful *reading.*

I have tried, in my books, to speak for thousands of American children, who are inarticulate and cannot speak for themselves. I speak for the under-privileged child, but also for the average American child, who though pampered and protected, still has problems to solve and situations to meet in his own life. I have tried to help the children of our country to understand each other better, by introducing those in one region to those in another. Our book-reading children come largely from our privileged groups and it is a disservice to them to let them grow up thinking all children are alike and have advantages like their own. Our book-reading children, who have few or no contacts outside their own class, should at least learn from books that there is poverty in the world, even in America, that homes are not always new and beautiful, filled with every luxury and comfort. They should learn that a home can be a mere framework for shelter, that there is sorrow as well as joy in the world, and that there are tragedies which even children must sometimes face. Above all, they should learn that life is always worth living, no matter what the circumstances, if it is met with courage and hope.

In traveling about our country I have tried to be a spokesman, an interpreter and a guide, introducing child readers to a variety of environments, and showing how children meet life and accept it. I believe that a book for the "middle-aged" child, from nine or ten upward, should be more than a pleasant conceit aimed to amuse and entertain and pass the time away. I believe that it should broaden their sympathies and compassion to include all kinds and conditions of men.

—Lois Lenski

Adventure in Understanding

HERE I LIVE

Here I live,
this is my home.
This very earth,
its richest loam
has grown my roots
and nurtured me.
Has given love,
security.
Here, being sent,
I am content.
My home is here,
I hold it dear.

A BOOK is always an adventure, whether into the known or the unknown. The primary purpose of a book is to communicate experience.

The three-year-old lives in a small home world. In it, everything is known and familiar—father and mother, brothers and sisters. He is surrounded by the warmth and kindness of his family, and by security within the four walls of home. His experience is not large. He is easily delighted by the simple happenings of everyday life—watching the rain, seeing a bird in a tree, helping mother sweep, eating three meals a day, going to bed at night, and getting up in the morning. There is drama to the three-year-old in these simple happenings, and their very repetition day after day makes them all the more dramatic.

And so books for the young child repeat these personal experiences. They convey the same simple facts and simple happenings which the child lives day after day. His books communicate his life, with all its wonder, beauty, humor, and simplicity. But the child grows and his world grows with him. He reaches out for new experiences and absorbs them. The first drawings that a child makes reflect his daily experiences and provide a reliable index into his thoughts and impressions.

I knew a small boy who was taken for the first time, one Sunday, to a cemetery. For weeks afterwards, every drawing that he made had a tombstone in it, with crude childish hieroglyphics on it. To this boy, the tombstone was a new experience, but it was readily absorbed and took its place in his habitual environment. Along with the houses, autos, flowers, clouds, and suns which he drew over and over, the tombstone found a happy place.

A little girl drew a picture of a house and put

sixteen chimneys on it. Of course, a literal-minded adult said to her: "But no house ever had 16 chimneys!" The child replied: "I'm drawing chimneys, not houses." She was expressing the idea "chimney." She had come to a complete comprehension of the experience "chimney" and had absorbed it as part of her life. Hence the appearance of multiple chimneys in her drawing.

As the young child grows, his curiosity develops and becomes a bridge from the known and the familiar out to the unknown and the unfamiliar. He begins to ask questions about the facts of the real world in which he lives. He wants to know how things work, what things are for, and where things come from. He keeps asking, "Why? Why? Why?" His questioning reflects a continual effort to understand the world, and so he enjoys factual books which answer these questions. His books center around things just a little outside his small home world. He likes stories about things that move—engines, boats, wagons with horses, airplanes. He likes stories about animals—real animals—what they eat, how to care for them, what they can be used for. He likes stories about other boys and girls who do the same things that he does.

While he is becoming grounded in basic facts, his imagination is also growing and developing. Then suddenly his imagination takes wings and soars, and mother becomes worried, because he goes through a period of what she calls "telling lies." What he is really doing is playing with facts. At first he may not know the difference between fact and fancy, and if this confused state continued, it might become dangerous, but with proper guidance, this is not likely to happen. Once he realizes the difference between fact and fancy, he enjoys the freedom of his wild imaginings because they are not bound down by fact. He enjoys them all the more because they are deviations from fact.

The period of enjoyment of make-believe is a glorious one—one of the happiest to share with any child or group of children. Make-believe and nonsense open the door to adventure in the vast field of folklore and fairy tales of every nation, as well as modern fanciful writing. They are a permanent part of children's literature. Make-believe fills a definite need at a certain stage in every child's development. It helps to feed his imagination, increase his creative activity, and stimulate his natural expressiveness.

In the imagination, anything can happen. All natural laws can be broken. A cow *can* jump over the moon, a giant's head *does* touch the sky, animals *can* talk and wear clothes! Anything can happen because you are playing with facts. Thus a fine sense of humor develops in imagining things that contradict facts. All playful variations from everyday truth become excruciatingly funny! And so the child eats up fairy tales and books of fancy and humor. This period comes earlier or later, and lasts for a longer or shorter time with different children.

While my son was small, I did everything I could to stimulate his imagination. I read him fairy-tales, I made up fanciful stories, I told him funny things to make him laugh. If a button came off his clothes and I sewed it on after he'd gone to bed at night, I told him next morning that the fairies had done it. I desperately wanted him to believe in fairies. I thought that every "literary" child would surely believe in fairies. But the harder I wished fairies on him, the less he would have to do with them. Did he believe in them? No. He thought they were silly, and he preferred realistic books.

I began to despair.

Finally, after I had completely given up hope, after I had concluded I had a completely unimaginative child, and after I let him go ahead choosing his own books, one day he found a fairy-tale that he liked. At the age of nine, which is rather late for it, he suddenly reached the fairy-tale age, and for two years, he read nothing else! For two years he would have nothing to do with realism and lived with his head in the clouds in a world that does not exist. Then he came back to real life again. But he has always retained the ability to enjoy fancy and humor, as do most children who are devotees of fairy-tales.

For there does come a time when the imagination loses its savor and its fascination fades. Make-believe does not satisfy a child's curiosity about life, and so he often finishes abruptly with it. He wants something real. He returns to the facts of the real world again. In school, his horizons widen. From the fourth grade on, he learns multitudes of facts of geography and history, of science and industry. The world is a complicated place. How can he understand it all?

Now, too, he notices that the world has people in it.

In babyhood, he was surrounded by the love

and devotion of his own family—by kind people. When a neighbor boy comes into the yard and snatches his toy from his hand, he learns for the first time that all people are not kind. Later in school, a boy knocks him down and gives him a black eye. His family is not there to protect him. He has to meet this situation himself. He sees other children doing mean and cruel things. His curiosity about people grows. Can it be there are bad people in the world? Reluctantly he has to admit that this is true.

But his experience remains limited in our standardized, mechanized world. Contacts with realities which were common enough to all children a generation ago, have been removed by the coming of the machine. Too many of our children, living in cities and larger towns, have no contact with animals, with the good earth and growing things, with the wonders of nature; they have no share in their parents' experiences of making a living. Their lives have become empty and barren of healthy, wholesome adventure. What is there for them to do out of school hours but dodge traffic, loaf at street corners, spend money, and feed upon comics, movies, and radio? If they turn to these other mediums for a synthetic excitement and adventure which is lacking in their own lives, who can blame them?

And so a child's reading becomes doubly important, for it must give him vicarious experience. Reading becomes a *great adventure in understanding*. First, it must give the child facts; second, it must interpret and evaluate those facts. The child must acquire knowledge, but more than that, he must learn to *comprehend* that knowledge. Knowledge is the mere acceptance of a fact by the mind. Comprehension goes much farther. Comprehension is grasping the meaning of the fact. As the dictionary says: to comprehend is to "embrace wholly within the mind."

A child's natural curiosity about life is one of his strongest characteristics, the one that has been least respected by adults. Children want to know about the mysteries of birth and death, of science and nature, of good and evil, of a thousand and one things which we adults keep veiled in mystery.

Books can widen a child's experience by opening up to him all the fascinating facts of biology, science, and nature, and help him to grasp the marvelous phenomenon that constitutes this world of ours. But they can do more than that. Facts are not enough. Facts are cold and dead unless they are interpreted, unless their meaning is understood. Books become a valuable guide to the child in fathoming the mysteries of a complicated world. They throw a shining light along his path that might otherwise lie in darkness.

Children learn in only two ways—through their own experience, and through the experiences of others; and so they must learn to understand people.

Children are naturally curious about people as they are about everything else. They want to know how people live and why. They want to know why they behave as they do, why some are good and others are bad. A child's actual knowledge of people is apt to be limited and distorted—colored by rumors, by gossip, by radio and movie contacts; and definitely conditioned by parental over-protectiveness. All too often, children have so little guidance, they become bored by the dullness of good people and intrigued by the glamour and daring of the wicked.

A book can be the most valuable sort of guide to the understanding of all kinds of people. And so it will not concern itself entirely with the bright and happy side of life. It will show the other side as well, presenting the sorrow and suffering that life brings to every human being. It is a fine thing for a child to know that there are good and honorable people in this world; that life is good and worth living. But this is only one side of the picture. Without the other, the child's vision is a blurred and distorted one. He should learn that man can be mean, unkind and despicable; that circumstances can warp and twist men's lives. He must learn that there is danger, peril, and tragedy in living, and they must be met with courage. Only when he realizes these things can he begin to understand other people and why they are what they are.

Only through a book is a child (or an adult) able to enter into the heart and mind of another person. A book can be a richer experience than life itself.

We all realize the inadequacy of personal experience. Two people standing face to face can be as far apart as the north and south poles, neither one knowing what the other is thinking or feeling. Our faces are masks to cover our thoughts. Our means of communication with each other are sadly inadequate—conversation, for instance. We talk and talk, but never arrive at a mutual sharing—an inner harmony—of ideas. I might talk to you for a week and never succeed in conveying to you the few simple truths which I want you to grasp. Our inability to express ourselves clearly, to convey our thoughts in speech and writing is pathetic. Words can mean so many things—there are so many shades of meaning. Only as people become more articulate, acquire the ability to put into words subtle differences of meaning, can they hope to live together harmoniously in spite of differences of opinion.

A book, as nothing else, can open the door to understanding between people. A book lays bare the hidden thoughts and motives, the hopes and ideals of a person who is outwardly different from ourselves, but, once we get inside his heart and mind, not so different either. He becomes a real brother in every sense of the word.

A book should *communicate experience* because so often, as with children of restricted experience, it becomes a substitute for life itself. A book character can be more real to a reader than a person he sees every day. The happenings in a book can be more vivid and more alive than those of the reader's real life. Because a book is a work of art, it is selective. It gives not only the outward facts and happenings themselves, reduced to their very essence, with all irrelevant trappings removed, but it presents also all the overtones and connotations which give these facts and happenings meaning. A book becomes a valuable commentary on human behavior. It gives a child help in evaluating people and experiences. Through reading, a child widens not only his knowledge—he absorbs the essential meanings involved. He *comprehends.*

In a book, a child identifies himself with the hero, thinks his thoughts, speaks as he speaks, acts as he acts—suffers his sufferings and rejoices in his joys. A book should communicate experience so vividly that a child, reading it, will *live* the book, and living it, will love it. Thus a book becomes an adventure in understanding.

Seeing Others as Ourselves

ME AND YOU

At first my world
was only ME,
Beyond
I could not see.
My life so small
I saw it all,
And when it changed
I never knew—
but I saw YOU.

I, myself and ME—
Beyond
I could not see.
My small world
grew.
It opened wide,
one came inside,
I looked and knew
that it was YOU!

WHAT A WONDERFUL country ours is! Wherever you go, you can always find new scenes, people with new customs and habits and different ways of making a living from those you have seen in other regions.

I think the artist is a specially privileged person, because, always he sees the world spread out like a stage before him, a play being enacted for his own special benefit. He approaches it objectively, with all his senses sharpened, filled with "a great awareness"—a sensitivity like that of a human camera, to make a record of it. He looks not for those things which are the same or similar to his own past experience, but for differences; he forgets himself and identifies himself with the new scene and its activities.

The approach of the artist and the writer is not exactly the same, even when they are one and the same person. An artist looks at the outward surface of things. He is primarily interested in what meets the eye. He looks for beauty, character, action, design and pattern, but he rarely goes more than skin-deep. The writer, on the other hand, has to understand reasons and motives. With all the inquisitiveness of a four-year-old, he keeps asking, "Why? Why? Why?" He must find out the hidden meanings beneath all he sees and hears.

What fun it is to explore a new and unknown world, full of limitless possibilities—of drama, human character and conflict, all the things that go to make up storytelling. The writer is blessed with a wonderful gift—the ability to enter a new world of people unlike any he has ever known, to bring to them an active sympathy, the outgrowth of his own past experience, to enter into their lives with understanding and to write of them *as if he were one of them.*

Marjorie Kinnan Rawlings says in her book, *The Golden Apples*:

> "There are worlds within worlds. It seemed to him a shocking thing that no man could see beyond the rim of his own. Perhaps there lay the ultimate wisdom, to see all life, all living, with the acute awareness one brought to one's own."

Sigrid Undset says the writer must have:

> "Insatiable curiosity toward other people's thoughts and towards horizons of undiscovered knowledge, the urge to identify oneself with others by imagination, until we suffer the sufferings of others and rejoice in their joys. These are the sources that feed our ideas about human solidarity, justice and pity and love and good-neighborliness."

We need to know our country better. We need to know not only our own region, where our roots are firmly put down, but other regions where live people different from ourselves—people of different races, faiths, cultures and backgrounds. We need to know native as well as foreign-born groups. I dislike the terms "minority groups" and "under-privileged peoples," because they imply superiority and condescension on the part of the person who uses them. I wish we could think of all men as people. When we know them, understand how they live and why, we will think of them as "people"—human beings like ourselves. Once we know them, we can say: "This is the way these people live. Because I understand it, I admire and love them." Even though they do not have bathtubs and electric washers, there is a great deal to admire and love.

I have often wished for an invisible cloak to wear, or at least a disguise, when I have gone visiting the Cajuns of Louisiana or the Crackers of Florida, so that I might become *one of them* and be accepted as such. But even then my speech and actions would betray me. It was very inconvenient, when gathering story material in the deep South, to look so much like a "Dam-Yankee!" But no—there was no other way. I had to go as myself—as an "outsider."

In the bayou country, you are an "American"; in the Cracker country, you are a "Yankee"; in the southern Appalachian Mountains, you are a "foreigner" or "from the outland"; and that is always a handicap. It is difficult for any "outsider" to be accepted and to share the deeper side of their lives. The surface, yes. They are all kind and curious and very human. But there is a barrier beyond which the outsider can rarely go—until he breaks it down.

A young Louisiana librarian, in advising me, said: "Well, if I wanted to get inside the Cajun homes, I'd go out and sell them something!" Strangely enough, although I wore no disguise, the children along the Louisiana bayous *did* ask me if I were selling something, because in one hand I carried a mysterious bag (containing lunch, purse, sketchbook, notebooks and camera) and in the other a campstool, without which no artist can ever travel. Always a crowd of children gathered, eager to watch a drawing grow on a sheet of paper—and eager to tell me many things I wanted to know. The children accepted me without question. Anyone who can draw pictures becomes their intimate friend. Wherever I went I always found a warm welcome because I drew pictures. My drawing helped, as nothing else could, to break down the barriers of suspicion. Drawing is a universal language which everybody understands.

Knowing the children was but a step toward knowing the adults. Soon their mothers were asking me to come and sit on the front gallery, or to come in the kitchen and have a cup of coffee. When you are invited to have coffee in Louisiana, you are no longer an "outsider." You are a friend. I shall never forget a memorable afternoon which I spent on a bayou bench, listening to an old French woman as she told me many incidents of her childhood and of three major floods through which she had lived.

Equally vivid is a morning spent in the Farmer's Market of a Florida town, sitting on an upturned orange crate behind the counter, listening while Old Man Dunnaway sang "Jaybird Sittin' on a Swingin' Limb" and other folksongs to me. On successive visits he told me the complete story of his boyhood. He was old and poor and uneducated, but his philosophy of life was one of the finest I have ever heard. He was a man to be admired and loved. When I bade him goodbye, before returning north, he grasped my hand in both his own and said: "I shall recollect you . . . in all pleasantness . . ."

From my first day in the mountains when I hitchhiked for six miles over a rough country road sitting on top of three sacks of grain in the back of a farmer's wagon, on my way to visit a blind chair maker, to the last day when I crossed Stone Mountain by train in a violent spring freshet, I met nothing but kindness in the mountains. I have never met a friendlier or more truly hospitable people. You are always asked, as you walk along a mountain road, to come in and rest a while. You are always invited to stay for the next meal or to spend the night. They say: "We haven't much, but what we have you're plumb welcome to!" One mountain woman told me she couldn't talk to anyone else as she could talk to me. She begged me to spend the summer with her and cried when I went away.

I met an old mountain granny on the street of a country town. She told me it was her first trip to town in six months. She carried a white meal sack over her arm, which contained purchases she had already made—a bag of seedbeans for her garden, a pair of new shoes and other things. I went with her on a search for a cast-iron frying pan. When at last she found it, the price was too high for her purse—or perhaps I should say for her pocket, for she carried her money in her blue-check apron pocket, firmly pinned shut with two large safety pins. And inside the pocket, the coins were wrapped in a man's size handkerchief and bound tightly around with a strong string. It was quite a complicated procedure to make a purchase, so I offered to pay for the frying pan. This was not generosity so much as a desire to witness her reaction. She hesitated, looked me over from head to foot, then decided to accept the gift. When I left her, eating a large boiled sweet potato taken from the inexhaustible meal sack, she said, "I don't know who you are, but you are a good woman. Come and see me and I'll fry chicken in that frying pan and give you all you can eat!"

And so, over and over again, I learned that fundamental lesson in living, that whatever you give comes back to you a hundred times over.

It is easy to see why a certain environment makes people live as they do, and affects every phase of their life—why in water-soaked Louisiana, where it is too wet to raise crops, the people make a living by fishing; and how in the dry sandy soil of Florida a struggle is necessary to grow oranges and strawberries; and how the simple farm life on steep hillsides has kept the mountain people cut off from the world. When we understand their environment and see how their lives have been conditioned thereby, then we can understand their behavior. We can imagine ourselves in the same situation, and we wonder if we would be different.

My own experience in getting stories from people who have lived them has been so rich that I have felt a strong desire to pass them on to others. It is my hope that young people, reading my regional books, will share the life of these people as I shared it, and living it vicariously, through the means of a vivid, dramatic, authentic, real-life story, will learn something of tolerance toward people different from themselves.

I am trying to say to children that all people are flesh and blood and have feelings like themselves, no matter where they live or how simply they live or how little they have; that man's material comforts should not be the end and object of life. I am trying to point out that people of character, people who are guided by spiritual values, come often from simple surroundings, and are worthy of our admiration and even our emulation.

Just as recent American painters no longer go to Paris for painting material, but have found here on our own doorstep a vivid, dramatic America which they are portraying not romantically or sentimentally, but realistically and truthfully, just so accurate regional books for children should present all the vividness and drama that the

American scene holds. We need not manufacture excitement—it is here, inherent in the scene itself. The way that Americans have struggled and fought and mastered their environment, in all its great variety, is an unending American saga.

Because these are true-to-life stories, I have included in my regional books certain incidents which we, as authors, following some unwritten taboos, have not often used in children's books. Our attitude, perhaps unconsciously, has been protective. We have felt that books for girls, at least, should be "nice," even though we have allowed somewhat stronger fare for boys. So, many of our girls' books have been pretty, sweet, and happy . . . and not much else.

I am writing for both boy and girl readers, and it has been my observation that our modern girls can take as strong fare as our boys. Children are getting exciting drama in many forms every day from other agencies, from the comics, the movies and the radio. Books must meet this competition, because anemic Pollyanna stories will only be shoved aside and not read at all.

We have not often put drunken fathers and malicious neighbors into a book for children. I have done this, and I would like to tell you why.

These incidents are a direct outgrowth of the environment which I have described. They are true and authentic. They have happened not once but a hundred times in this particular locality, and have been experienced by the children as well as by the adults. To leave them out and to pretend that such things never happen would be to present a false picture. I could not blindfold my own eyes. I could not close my ears when Cracker children told me of quarrels with their neighbors caused by open range law for cattle and hogs. I became keenly interested in learning how the finer people among the Crackers met such happenings and reacted to them. I was amazed to discover that after some of their worst fights, the quarreling neighbors came together for an evening frolic or a neighborhood square dance, forgetting their differences. They seemed to be taking an initial step in learning how to live together, in spite of differences of opinion.

I have always believed that children are strongly affected by their parents' way of life and by everything that happens to them. There are, unfortunately, many drunken fathers and objectionable neighbors in the world, and there are many children, whether we like to believe it or not, who have to face these facts and do something about it, as Birdie and Shoestring did.

There are also more fortunate children who have never come in contact with facts of this kind. I believe it will do the latter no harm to widen their horizons a bit, and let them know that such conditions exist. Our present-day attitude toward children—that a child should live a completely sheltered life, have no cares, no responsibilities, no knowledge of the existence of pain, sorrow and trouble—may well be questioned.

After all, these boys and girls in the upper grades are now preparing to meet life as adults. In ten years time they will be voters. Why shouldn't they know something about the country they live in? And the different kinds of people who live in it? Why shouldn't they begin to think a little?

I have been dwelling at length on my purpose behind this series of regional books. My approach, however, is not that of the propagandist or even of the humanitarian. It is that of the artist. To enjoy a work of art is to live more intensely, to see, through the artist's interpretation, a deeper meaning in the commonplace. And so a book of this kind should need no explaining. I do not believe we need deliberately to preach or teach in a story book. Children are so quick to respond. If a book tells a vital human-interest story, children will quickly pick up the overtones. We need not ram it down their throats.

A book about a strange people should be as vital an experience as meeting these people face to face. It should do more than that—it should enable the reader to get beneath the skin of the strange person, to stand in the strange person's shoes, to *be* that person in imagination. What better way, than through the reading of a book, to enter the minds and hearts of others and find them full of good things? What better way to learn to love our neighbor as ourself? Only when we truly *see others as ourselves* can we hope to have a world in which all men are brothers.

I cannot conclude without a word as to the speech or dialect used in these books. We have as many different kinds of American speech as we have regions. It is interesting to study the different ways the American language is used. Speech is so much more than words—it is poetry, beauty, character, emotion. To give the flavor of a region, to suggest the moods of the people, the atmosphere of the place, speech cannot be overlooked. When I remember the soft, velvety tones of the bayou-French people, the way they transfer our English words into their native French rhythm, when I hear again the soft, lazy drawl of the Florida Crackers or the mountain people with fine old forgotten Elizabethan phrases on their lips, it seems to me sacrilege to transfer their speech to correct, grammatical, school reader English, made easy enough for the dullest child to read. To me, this would be a travesty on all the beauty and character in the lives of these people.

Words, as listed in the dictionary, are dead. Words become alive only with use. A coat takes on the character of a man after he has worn it and shaped it to his person—it becomes truly his, and reflects his personality. Until words are used they are dead and lifeless. Through use, words become *living speech,* echoing the spirit within. Words need to be "worn" to attain beauty. There is poetry in the common speech of man.

The sound of a horse's hoofs pounding on a country road makes a beautiful and a satisfying rhythm. The noises of nature—the caw of the crow as it flies over the field, the buzz of the bee, the hum of the locust—all these have their rhythm.

And so does the speech of the human being. In New England we hear one rhythm, in Louisiana another, in Florida and the mountains another. In the simplest words, with only a minimum of distortions in spelling, this is what I have tried to convey. There may be some children who will find it difficult reading. But I am willing to make that sacrifice, because of all that those who *do* read it will gain, in the way of understanding "the feel" of a different people, and the "flavor" of a life different from their own.

If these books should help only a few children to "see beyond the rim of their own world" and gain that "ultimate wisdom," I shall be rewarded.

Regional Children's Literature

A BOOK CAN TAKE ME

A book can take me
out and away,
To another world,
to another day;
To another life
I have never known,
To another life
unlike my own.

A book can open
for me a door
To another life
unknown before;
A book can give me
understanding new,
Of people and places
my whole life through.

We are grateful to Wendell Wilkie for giving us the phrase One World. He meant, as we all know, that we must learn to live as brothers to make the world "One." We have now many separate worlds, little worlds with fences between, fences so high we cannot see over them. Each of us thinks that *our* world is the only one. We do not know or understand other people's worlds, beyond our own fence. Before we can hope to understand foreign nations and life at peace with them, we must understand our own country and the different kinds of people who live in it.

Regional art, painting and literature, is, basically speaking, the presentation of a *way of life* in a certain region which has developed or preserved in itself a certain homogenous individuality. Because of the great diversity of setting and of types of people in our country, it is practically impossible to write of it as a whole, as a national entity. We have our New England, our South, our Middle West, our Far West, and under these divisions, many more subdivisions and groups. And so any sound understanding of our country as a whole becomes an understanding of its component parts.

Regional art in America is a fairly recent development. Only a generation ago it was considered necessary for an artist to study painting in Paris. American art schools were not good enough; or, if an artist started in them, he had to finish in Paris. He had to paint European landscapes, he had to paint in a European manner. Certain subjects were considered "artistic," other subjects were taboo, among them, machinery or locomotives, mechanical or industrial subjects, ugly and sordid subjects, especially anything that smacked of realism. Art in the Paris tradition was romantic, sentimental to varying degrees, artistic, but it had little relation to real life.

It took considerable courage for a few men to break away and to find America worth painting. Outstanding examples are three—Grant Wood of

Iowa, John Stewart Curry of Kansas and Thomas Hart Benton of Missouri. Along with their choice of American subject matter, these men developed also a more forthright technique, painting with directness, simplicity and vividness. At the same time that this regional American art was developing, American literature was doing the same thing. Theodore Dreiser, Erskine Caldwell, Willa Cather and others were finding America worth writing about and writing of it simply, directly and vividly.

Regional art, painting or literature, can be produced by: first, a native son or daughter, or second, by an outsider.

The native son, who has his roots there, should be by all means the best interpreter of his own region. There are many fine examples of authors who have done this. I think particularly of Sara Orne Jewett and her fine stories of New England and New England character. Among our juvenile authors we have Marguerite d'Angeli of Pennsylvania, May Justus of Tennessee, Will James of the cow country, Laura Ingalls Wilder of the prairie country and many others.

But often the native son has limitations. He is too close to the scene, he "cannot see the forest for the trees." Sometimes too he is ashamed of his own background and beginnings. He wants to go *somewhere else* to find something to paint or write about. The native son may know the scene so well he cannot get outside of it and see it with perspective. For example, Grant Wood had to go to France and Italy first and learn that they held nothing for him, before he was ready to come back to Iowa and see what his own state offered him. One's own autobiography is always the hardest book to write, because the details are all too personal and it hurts too much to write objectively of them.

The outsider, coming into a region new to him, has the great advantage of having "eyes to see," he has a greater receptivity because of the newness of the scene—it has never had a chance to grow stale to him. He has, perhaps, a stronger desire to assimilate the new scene.

It was, of course, as an outsider that I gathered the material for my three first regional books, *Strawberry Girl, Bayou Suzette* and *Blue Ridge Billy*. I did not deliberately set out to travel in search of book material, but I have always found material, crying out to be recorded, on every doorstep where I have set my foot. Those who have "eyes to see" never run out of subject matter for creative expression.

Some fifteen years ago, I, Ohio born and bred, went to live in Connecticut in an old 1790 farmhouse. Before I consciously realized what was happening, I was learning Connecticut history from my neighbors and I was starting a series of books for children with Connecticut and New England historical backgrounds. Incidentally I also started to paint a series of portraits of my rural Connecticut neighbors—a gallery of "Connecticut Yankees"—but my books soon began to absorb all my time, and this ambitious project had to be abandoned! The writing of these books was forced upon me, the material was lying there on my doorstep—"treasure for the taking." I could not sidestep it, although outwardly this little Connecticut town was no different from any other and not spectacular in any way. Many authors or artists might have passed it by and said there was nothing there.

But the experience of writing teaches us over and over again one important lesson, that there is a story in every human being. How many stories then can a small town offer—if we have the time to pause, the eyes to see, and the hearts to understand.

Later, it so happened that because of ill health, my doctor advised my spending my winters in a warmer climate. I went first to Louisiana and spent a winter in New Orleans, where I was confronted with stories on all sides. There was the exciting history of old New Orleans, the charm of the French Quarter, the fascination of the colored children—a thing to be constantly resisted—and there was the real life I saw being lived by French-speaking people in the rural regions along the bayous, especially the life of the children there. I had to put it into a book, I couldn't help myself. It was there waiting for me.

When I found out what an exciting life the Louisiana children live, I wanted to go right home to Connecticut and tell the children there about it. Then I went to Florida and learned that children live still different lives in that land of sunshine and orange trees and strawberries. Why don't we know more about our own country? Why shouldn't the children of Louisiana and Florida and Connecticut and other parts of the country get to know each other? Why haven't Louisiana writers told us how Louisiana people live? Why haven't Florida writers told us how Florida people live? If the native sons and daughters have not "eyes to see," why should not an outsider do it?

And so I found myself writing regional books for children, and through the process, I have developed an insatiable curiosity about how other people live.

To write these books, I went to live with the people in these regions, to really get to know them first-hand. I talked with them, ate and drank with them, sat in their kitchens and on their porches, and always I listened as they told their experiences. The children told me a great deal and so did their parents. I took my sketch book with me, and made drawings of the people, their houses, their furnishings and many details of their surroundings. If any one was suspicious of me as an outsider, I did not know it. My drawings helped me, as nothing else could, to make friends of complete strangers. Children crowded round me like flies, eager to watch a drawing grow on a sheet of paper, devoted friends after the first stroke.

It is easy to win the confidence of people if your approach is fundamentally sympathetic, if you show a kindness that is real, not affected, and if you can forget your own life, your own background, and put yourself wholeheartedly into their point of view in all their trials and experiences. Most people like to talk of themselves and talk best under the stimulus of a sympathetic audience. I am the best listener in the world: I never interrupt!

It is a wearing and an exhausting experience, both physically and spiritually, to become "one of them," to live in imagination with people who are different from any you have seen or known before, but it is a rewarding experience as only creative activity can be.

Children often ask me if my stories are true, and my characters real. I call these regional books "true-to-life," because for most of the characters in them, I had living persons in mind. Birdie Boyer in *Strawberry Girl* is a real little girl I saw plowing in a sandy field in Florida. Little did I dream when I snapped her photograph and talked to her, that she would make friends for me all over the country and return to me nearly three years later, bearing the Newbery Medal in her hand! So when I am asked if my characters are real, I feel I can honestly say yes.

Because of its very nature, regional literature for children becomes a challenge, a challenge to authors to interpret our regions with insight and understanding, and a challenge to those of us who use books, to understand their fundamental purpose and thus help in the important task of widening understanding among different groups.

A regional book shows how a way of life is controlled by an environment. It shows how people live in a certain region and why they live as they do and how outward circumstances have made them live as they do. It will emphasize unimportant outward differences, but it will also emphasize the inward universal likenesses in behavior.

A book is always a vicarious experience. This is particularly true for a child, who identifies himself with the hero of a book in an astonishing way, because of the tremendous power of his imagination. In a book about a horse, the child *becomes* the horse. In a book about a dog, he *is* the dog. In the same way, an adult or child lives with the hero or heroine of a novel, thinks with him, suffers and rejoices with him, speaks and acts like him, understands and loves him.

Surely we all realize the inadequacy of personal experience. Two people, standing face to face, can be as remote as the north and south poles. How often, standing before him, you have not the slightest clue to what the other person is thinking.

Faced with a strange person, a strange scene or situation, an unfamiliar experience, we are apt to be suspicious or to laugh defensively. After we get to know the strange person, we are surprised to learn that he has two eyes, two ears as we have. He has two arms, two legs, even a heart and a mind. He is no longer a misunderstood monster, but a human being like ourselves, with faults and frailties, similar to our own, but also with our own feeble goodness, our own faith in the right, in justice and in truth. How can this metamorphosis come about? How can this unfamiliar monster be changed into a human being?

One of the best ways is through books. This is about the only way that children—or adults—can get a vivid glimpse into the inner life and thought-processes of a strange person—by sharing it in a book. This is made possible because the author has studied, sympathized with and loved these people, shared their life, become "one of them," and by his gifts of creation and imagination has laid the strange person's thoughts, emotions, motives and intentions bare before the reader—*and they are not very different from the reader's own.*

I believe that children should be constructively taught a sympathetic approach to the strange person, and by the phrase "strange person" I mean any person different from themselves in race, color, creed or background. Without such teaching, children are apt to follow the crowd like sheep; they think in herds, because they haven't the courage for independent thinking and action. They are thoughtless—they can torture a newcomer in their group who is different in speech, in clothing or in habits. But I do not believe for a minute that they have basically cruel or barbaric tendencies. When they perpetrate cruelties, it is either the result of adult example, or they do it out of thoughtlessness or lack of imagination. They do not realize how it hurts the other person. They have never learned to put themselves in the other person's place. This shows their great need of guidance, of books which stress the inward thinking of different kinds of people.

Children need to be told that we want to keep differences in speech, in habits, in personality. Why should we all dress alike, talk alike, think alike, act alike? The world would be a stupid place if we did. It is all these racial and regional differences that make our country so unique. Our country has always stood for the widest kind of cosmopolitanism.

We want to encourage a pride in our own locality, a pride in our own local, colorful use of the American language, and a pride in the particular cultural heritage which our group has contributed. Instead of emphasizing these differences between groups to deliberately separate and bring hostility between them, we want to look upon them as a valuable heritage. We want to encourage also a pride in those universal qualities which are common to all groups and which can help us to live harmoniously together. The magnificent thing is that out of so many backgrounds and heritages, there exist so many similarities and likenesses if we will only look for and acknowledge them.

We must never forget that among all men there exist a response to the beautiful, the love of home and family, the fear of insecurity, the appreciation of sacrifice, the desire for personal achievement and the longing to be at one with the universe. These are universal experiences, these are the bonds which hold men together. If good were not dominant in the world, the human race would have destroyed itself long ago.

There used to be a time, not so long ago, when the little home, the little farm in this country was self-sufficient and self-contained—a safe little world in itself. But the automobile and enlarged means of communication have changed all that. People now leave their own backyards and, in the family car, travel thousands of miles into other regions than their own. They see people living in all sorts of different ways they never thought possible before. Southerners come north, northerners go south, easterners go west, westerners come east. The traveler comes home, and he remembers those other regions, those other homes so different from his own, that other people love just as dearly as he loves his own. He becomes a new person, a person with a wider vision. He comes to only one conclusion—here is our great, wide, beautiful country, with room enough for all, for many kinds of people. We need not all be alike, we must not all be alike. We must hold fast to our individuality, but our local patriotisms can be cherished without any conflict between them. And so, loving my own little corner, where my roots are put down, becomes a part of loving the whole, a part of a true tolerance for all those other people in their backyards.

In regional books for children, then, we stress a particular environment and the way of life which it has brought into being. By understanding this environment, we learn *why* the people speak, think and act as they do. We realize that under the same circumstances, we would speak, think and act the same as they do. And so we come to understand a basic concept behind all experience—the universality of human behavior. The most important lesson that any child—or adult—has to learn is the ability to put himself in the other person's place.

And so we need to hold our banner high, the banner of unselfishness, of genuine love for others, and of faith in our fellow men. This may be a dark and a confused and a complicated age through which we are passing, but there are certain eternal verities as true today as they have always been. Let us hold on to them. Let us hold them up as a lighted candle in a dark place. Fortunate, indeed, are we who work with children. In their world, there is always joy, beauty and hope. There is constant faith, trust and respect for all. Work with and for children is always constructive, building for the future—building One World.

Are your Books True?

WALK THE EARTH GENTLY

Walk the earth gently,
Step light, step light;
Lest snail or beetle
Be shorn of delight.

Walk the earth gently,
Nor linger nor stay;
Lest grass, blade or flower
Perish away.

Walk the earth gently,
Go slow, go slow;
Hurt not the stranger
You never will know.

OVER AND OVER again the children ask me: "Are your books true? Are the characters real?" In whatever part of the country I go, whenever I talk to children, this question never fails to come up.

Of *Strawberry Girl* they ask: "Was there really a boy named Shoestring and did he really throw a snake on Birdie's hat?" When I tell them yes, that I actually saw him and talked to him and sketched him, their faces beam with delight and *Strawberry Girl* takes on new meaning.

I remember a sixth grade in Kansas, who were most insistent on getting at the truth behind *Blue*

Ridge Billy. They had to be assured that in North Carolina there is a real store with one leg resting on a stone in a real Roundabout Creek, and that I saw it myself. When I told them that I had bought a pair of shoe-strings from the cross bachelor store-keeper as an excuse to talk to him, and that I had seen his unmade bed in the back corner with my own eyes, they sighed blissfully and said, "So that's how it was. We just knew you didn't make it up."

Of *Cotton in My Sack,* the children keep asking: "Did you really go there and pick cotton? Was there a real shotgun house and do they really paste newspapers on the walls to keep warm in winter?" The best way to answer them is to show them a photograph of myself with sunbonnet on my head and a cotton sack slung round my shoulder, and another of the Hutley's real shotgun house standing in the cotton field. Then they believe me.

I read the manuscript of *Judy's Journey* aloud to a group of seventh grade children from a neighboring Connecticut town. One chapter brings out the fact that the migrant children cannot go to the movies because they have no money. The children asked me: "Is it true? Are there any children in the United States so poor they cannot go to the movies? We thought all the poor children were in Europe." To them, the idea of poor children in America was incredible. In their own experience in a prosperous manufacturing town in Connecticut, they had never seen poverty. And although they had a good reading background, they had never encountered poverty in books. This fact made it all the more important for me to write this book.

I discussed with them the whole matter of truth in books and they were unanimous in their decision that a "true-to-life" story should be really true. They said, "If there are poor children in our country, we want to know how they live and why they are poor." An eighth grade girl asked me: "What can we do about it?"

Once a group of children from the cotton section of Arkansas wrote me why they liked *Strawberry Girl* so much. They said:

> "So many things in the story have happened to us. Your books are the only ones we have read that are about real children. They do lots of the same things that we do."

Other children have written me, saying:

"I dont know much when it comes to books, but I know what I like to read. I like to read about real boys and girls. I like books that have adventure and have boys and girls talk the way they really do, the way they would talk to any one." John, Grade 6.

"The kind of books I like best of all are stories of adventure about different places, places we never hear much about. I like to hear how different people live, what they do for a living, what crops they raise and what kind of house they live in." David, Grade 5.

"Many books could stand much more excitement,instead of just one thing happening and then it turns out that the people lived happily ever after. Why couldn't a few books end having the characters die?" Jannette, Grade 7.

"I like a story to have characters that are like us and have paper routes, they have their difficulties and fun too." Harold, Grade 8.

When they ask, "Are your books true?" the children are so serious and earnest in their questioning, *they want it to be true so badly*, that I would feel guilty and somewhat ashamed if I had to admit it was all make-believe. Under their insistence, truth seems to become, as it should be, tremendously important.

When *Prairie School* was published—probably the truest story I have ever written—again the children asked, "Is it true? It sounds like it happened in the olden days, a hundred years ago. Did this really happen in 1949?" A certain newspaper reviewer was skeptical also. He made this statement: "We are asked to believe that all this happened in one winter and to one family." Yes, we are asked to believe it, because it did happen to one family in one winter, and it is all an understatement of the real facts. How strange it is that, given the truth, we are unwilling to recognize and accept it.

About the same time, a twelve-year-old girl wrote me from Detroit saying she thought *Prairie School* was the best book she had ever read. She added: "I suppose it was not true, but it seemed like it." "I suppose it was *not* true, but it seemed like it." She liked it so much, she wanted it to be true. Other children showed skepticism. They asked me: "Did you make all this up in your head? Did you just imagine it all?" What they want to know is: "Can we trust this book, or is it ALL FAKE?"

It seems an amazing thing that an author should have to stand up and defend the truth. Is it because children are getting so much falsity, exaggeration and distortion from all sides that they are rebelling instinctively against it? Is their natural instinct for honesty and truth asserting itself? I believe it is, and I say: "More power to them!"

It is a sad and tragic thing if children are losing their faith in books—if they believe that what they read in story books is not true. It would be good to hear children say: "That's true. I read it in a book." But alas! Too often they are saying: "I read it in a book, but of course I knew it wasn't true." Or, like the girl from Detroit: "I suppose it was not true, but it seemed like it was." Instinctively, she wanted the truth. These groping questions make a thoughtful author pause and consider. Are we betraying a trust?

What have we been giving children in books? Anne Thaxter Eaton has defined good books for children as "books that will open a door, first, into a world of wonder and beauty and high imagination; second, into a world of reality and great people; and third, into a world of fun, nonsense and humor as well as a world of deep seriousness." Of all these areas, the second has been the most neglected—the area of reality and great people.

There has always been considerable accent on the fanciful, the nonsensical and the preposterous. I believe in fancy and I want some of it for every child, but not an exclusive diet. I believe in the imagination, for without it, no author would be able to project himself into the life and thought of another person. But when fancy is confused with reality, it becomes definitely harmful. When children confuse truth with reality, when children cannot recognize truth when they see it—as in "I suppose it was *not* true, but it seemed like it,"—then something is wrong somewhere. And when fancy or the miraculous takes over completely in our so-called true-to-life stories, there is genuine cause for alarm.

We may well object to books which masquerade as real-life stories, books which uphold a vicious snobbery of wealth or position, books with synthetic, concocted plots which have no truth or existence save in the author's mind, and which can only give children false ideas of living. Such books are bad because they treat of an unreal world, not the world of true fancy, where children know they are having fun imagining things, but an unreal world which pretends to be the one in which children live. This type of book can only confuse and harm them. It can never help them to face the problems of their own adulthood.

Children would not keep on asking "Is it true?" if their books satisfied them. This must be because too many of their books give an untrue picture of real life and children instinctively sense it. Perhaps we have built up in books a synthetic world which never existed, in an effort to protect children from the harshness of the real world that does exist, or to pretend it is not there at all. But this is subterfuge and children do not want to accept it. They want the real thing. They want the truth.

Children live in a real world. There is excitement, drama and tragedy in the everyday life of thousands of children. In many parts of the country it has been my good fortune to share with them some of their experiences. I have found them in rural schools, in strawberry, corn and cotton fields, by stream, river and bayou, on steep mountain hillsides and on the unending rolling prairie. I have found them on street corners and in slums and apartment houses in towns and cities.

I have been more deeply moved by stories which children have told me of their real-life experiences than by any novel I have ever read. I have studied their faces as they have told me how tragedy touched them. They tell of the death of a pet dog, a mother's fatal illness, of caring for a sick horse or cow as of a commonplace. They take life as it comes, showing amazing courage. Sharing their tragedies with one who cares eases the pain. They share their joy, their gladness, their humor too. Each is a part of living.

A study of children themselves and the real lives they live can provide the richest kind of book material, books from which other child readers will learn something of the art of living, books which may help to satisfy children's groping instinct for more truth. It puts a responsibility on the author, to interpret for them the truth of everyday living. In recent years, the subject matter in adult books has been widened to include all aspects of life. Just so must the horizon in children's books widen to include many subjects that are now taboo.

In real life, a child can *never* change the economic situation of the family, or take them from poverty to sudden riches. And besides, are sudden riches so desirable after all? But in real life, a child's character can grow and develop, it can be shaped and changed by circumstances and by human relations. A book, by insisting on truth, can show those things that influence a child's character, and how a changed attitude on the part of a child can help his family face a crisis. A child's perennial hope—and even the child in the most abject surroundings glories in hope—can always be a worthy theme for a book.

Thomas Wolfe said: "We are the sum of all the moments in our lives; all that is ours is in them; we cannot escape or conceal it. Fiction is not fact, but it is fact selected and understood. It is fact arranged and charged with purpose."

There is no question as to what children like, first, last and always. They continually hunger and thirst after an interpretation of life itself. They are not satisfied with evasions, but want the real thing. And so they keep asking in a loud chorus: "Are your books true? Are your books true?"

How far can we go when we present life itself to children?

Dr. Arthur T. Jersild, Prof. of Education at Teachers College, Columbia, once said: "Much of what is done in education is an evasion rather than a way of facing problems that occur in the lives of children." He added: "Children learn to bound the States of the Union and memorize the names and dates of bygone wars. They study the habits of beavers, they learn about the distant stars and the antics of Mother Goose. But the subject of human behavior, human motives and the inner life of man has been pretty much ignored in our schools."

He recommended ways in which the child "might achieve and attain a healthy understanding of himself and others and a wholesome attitude of self-acceptance." He suggested that the child "develop a capacity for making allowances for others when they are peevish or irritable;" that the child "develop the ability to see through some of the arts and dodges, masquerades, concealments and camouflages of human motives, including his own." If this should be the aim of education, why should it not also be the aim of good books? Why should not real people be put into books, so that children may learn to understand and love them?

Do children really want books about the Elsie Dinsmores and the Pollyannas, about goody-goody heroes and heroines? We tried that in the early nineteen hundreds. Children read them then because there was nothing else to read. I read them as a child. I wept my eyes out over Elsie Dinsmore and her cruel father and over *The Wide Wide World,* a book filled with mawkish sentiment and heavy moralizing. Will children read them now? Very few. They will stop at the second page of *Little Lord Fauntleroy.* The children of today have been brought up on more wholesome fare. They find such stories boring, they hate stories with an obvious moral. They know the perfect hero is not true, not real.

But we authors are still moralists at heart. We still want to make our children good, if not better; but we do it in a different way. We do it not by precept but by example. We show often faulty or questionable behavior and we let the child reader evaluate it and draw his own conclusions.

A question arises. If we put questionable characters and ungrammatical speech or local idiom into a book, are we harming the child reader? Is he going straight out and copy it? I have never heard of a single instance where a child learned bad speech from reading it in a book, or learned bad conduct from reading of a bad hero. Such examples are more apt to work the other way.

They are apt to help him to evaluate the hero's conduct, and then go on to think about and judge his own. Heroes are not put into books to serve as models of perfection. They are put there as examples of human beings to help make a child think.

I wrote one book about a very selfish little girl, but the word *selfish* is never mentioned in the text. In reading *Texas Tomboy* aloud, in manuscript, to a group of fourth and fifth graders, I listened to their comments. They said: "Charlie Boy wasn't very thoughtful." "She wanted everything for herself." "She wasn't fair to her older sister, Grace." When she rode her pony across the neighbor's field just for spite, the children were furious. "Oh!" they cried: "She shouldn't do that! She's *mean!*" One boy applied the lesson to his own life. He said, "One time I did something just as mean as that. I deliberately rode my bike over our neighbor's flower bed!" As Charlie Boy's misbehavior continued, this same boy said in disgust: "Oh! I just wish she'd get what's coming to her!"

For perhaps the first time, they were judging a book character. They were able to see selfishness objectively, the first step in evaluating their own conduct, by seeing that selfishness never pays. It hurts the selfish one and others too, a valuable concept for any child to acquire from the reading of a book. Young readers *love* Charlie Boy because they feel she is a human being with faults like their own, not a model of perfection, but a girl of character and courage. They rejoice when she is able to overcome her selfishness for a larger end—which is not an impossible miracle at all.

How far can we go in putting realism into a book? The word *realism* has acquired a bad connotation, because many adult novelists have put the accent on depravity and degeneracy, which is as bad as accent on Pollyanna goodness. The question remains: Should the child be shielded in his books from sadness and sorrow, from evil and wickedness, from hurting and being hurt, from killing and dying, from pain, tragedy and violence—in other words, from the unpleasant side of life?

My own answer is that the scope of life covered in children's books needs to be greatly widened. It seems a natural thing for a child to read about all sorts of living. You cannot separate living and dying, or good and evil in the same person. Joy has a meaning to a child only in proportion as sadness is comprehended. Such topics, presented sympathetically as a part of the honest pattern of life as it comes to us all, can prepare a child for adulthood, when, in these disturbed times, violence may face him in every day's newspaper. By reading of the hurts of others, will not a child be better able to meet his own?

But even if greater and more honest realism comes into children's books, I believe they will always remain constructive and positive in their total effect, that they will reveal a genuine love of life and elevate the human spirit. Sordidness for its own sake, or played up as sensationalism, as done in so many of our novels, will be out of place. Life has its difficulties, yes—but man has the courage to meet it.

Such books will help the child to feel with others and to project himself into the lives of others—the ultimate purpose of true religion and true democracy. The child needs to see others as human beings, not as oddities or eccentrics, or as beings to fear, reject or look down upon, or as creatures to feel superior to. He needs to accept and understand differences in people and to see underlying reasons for these ways. He needs to feel a vital kinship with all sorts of people. The child needs to leave his own safe, narrow, little world and to venture forth in a true understanding of the ways of others. What better goal can there be for a book than to widen a child's horizons?

It is good to have one's roots buried deep in one's home place, in the place where you were born. It is good to read a book about the life we ourselves know well. So often we say: "How good this book is! It tells exactly what *I* think." What should we ask of a story—that it shall illuminate life only as we know it? Yes, and also life as we do not know it. It should take us far beyond the life we know.

Then our feeling will be: "How strange this is! I never thought of that before, and yet I see that it is true. Now that I know these people's problems, I can understand them better. I can see why they behave as they do. I would do the same if I were in their place." And so a book becomes a door, an open door to wider understanding. It helps the child to widen his experience, to go places he cannot go in real life, to understand people he has never seen and who behave differently from the way he does. But when a book takes him inside the hero's heart and mind, he finds he is not so different either. In fact, the book has made him *so real*, the child says: "He seems just like my brother."

The word *realism* needs to be rescued from an implication of sordidness. A new, tender and understanding realism can take its place, especially in the realm of children's books. A realism which recognizes the struggles people face, the battles they fight, the courage they bring to them, often against great odds, the sorrows they bear as well as the happiness they enjoy. I would like to see in children's books a stronger accent on a true and balanced realism, which recognizes the worth and dignity of every human being.

I once asked some children: "Is there too much unhappiness in this story?" They replied with an emphatic, "NO! Life is not all happy." We discussed whether or not a book should always have a happy ending. They said, "No, because in real life things do not always end happily." Then one little girl added wistfully, "But I think it should be hopeful. It should end on a note of hope." She had put the whole thing in a nutshell. How wise children are! They are never destructive in their thinking. They have faith and they live in hope. Everything is possible to them.

In children's books we can present glimpses of common behavior which will help us all to feel more akin. Let us give children the truth for which they are instinctively seeking. Let us say to them, "Yes, my books are true."

Getting Books from Life

GO TRAVEL A NEW LAND

Go travel a new land,
Push open the tight-closed door;
Go walk a path of strangeness
You have not walked before.

Go travel a new land
And look for a welcome there;
Go walk a path of strangeness
With people who love and care.

Go travel a new land
With eyes and ears and heart;
Go make it your own land,
A land of yourself a part.

THERE ARE three sources of literature:

First, books come from the imagination. Many of our books for children are made up in the mind of the author. The author sits at his desk and invents or imagines characters, incidents and happenings which he thinks will entertain, instruct or amuse his readers. Such books are entirely fictional.

Second, books come from other books. Through research into records left by past generations, many authors re-create events and happenings of the past. These historical books are second-hand, because the author did not himself experience them. Often such books are based on insufficient or inadequate knowledge of past life, so they too become largely fictional. Even biographies which make use of all known facts regarding their subject are often treated fictionally.

Third, books come from life itself.

Getting books from life itself is such a wonderful experience that I could wish all authors might have it. In a way, it is like "casting bread upon the waters," for whatever you give comes back a hundredfold. I would not change my basic approach to writing—going to real people to get my stories—even if I could. And I find now that it is impossible for me to change it. Unless I can see the setting of the story in my mind's eye, unless I can visualize my characters—people whom I have known in the flesh—I find I cannot write the story. I have gotten so far away from the invented, fabricated, imaginary stories which I first wrote, that I could not and would not want to go back to that type of writing.

I wish I could share with you a few high-spots of my experiences in getting material for my Regional books. Where shall I take you—to the mountains, the bayous, the plains or the prairies? What a wonderful country ours is, with so many different kinds of people of all nationalities, so many different faiths, races, cultures and backgrounds. A country of hills and mountains, of prairie and seashore; wet, dry, windy, cold and hot climates; all kinds of conditions, all kinds of occupations and environments to determine the way people get their living, to shape their lives and character.

My Regional books are an attempt to tell about some of these people, to give children a broader and more sympathetic understanding of people different from themselves, one little but important step on the way to the brotherhood of man. I first wrote of the bayou-French of Louisiana, then of the Crackers of Florida and the mountain people of North Carolina. From then on I received and accepted invitations from the cotton children of Arkansas, the prairie children of South Dakota and the corn-farm children of Iowa.

One book has led to another. The fact that American children are carrying on this series has been very gratifying to me. I do not arbitrarily choose a location. I wait until I am led or guided to it. When the people of a community want to be written about, I can be sure of complete cooperation. One of the most wonderful things about getting material for my books is the generous help I receive from everybody. The people in my books are real people whom I have known and loved, not just figments of my imagination.

The hard part about writing a true story is making people believe it is true. Even editors who publish probably ten fictional books to one real-life book assume you have "made up" an incident. When it sounds a bit improbable to them, be cause of their limited experience, they think it is your mistake and could not be true. They find many real life incidents "unconvincing." Even though they allow all kinds of fantastic happenings in a work of fiction, many real-life incidents are questioned.

Children, too, doubt that a story can be really true, and automatically assume it has no basis in fact. Because so many of the books they read are fictional or fantastic, they have acquired the false notion that all stories are made up. While they desperately want to believe that a story they love is true, they feel sure it cannot be. The more they love it, the more sure they are that it cannot be true. Even when I tell them it is, I can still see doubt in their eyes.

This brings out the difference between a story of real life and fiction.

It is interesting to investigate the meaning of the word *story*. Originally, according to Webster, a story was "a connected narration of that which has occurred; an account or recital of some incident or event." Before the age of printing, stories were recounted by word of mouth and often became exaggerated in the telling. "A story" became "a tale." The word "tale" meant a fictitious narrative—in other words, a true story that had been somewhat embroidered or magnified.

Hence, the final meaning of the word *story*, as listed by Webster, is: "a fib, a lie or a falsehood." Then Webster adds: "a euphemism used chiefly by and to children."

"Oh, you told a story!" says one child to another, meaning falsehood. Mothers become alarmed when children embroider facts with fancy, and so the word *story* has fallen into disrepute. Originally it meant a recounting of "that which actually happened." Now it usually means fiction. Can it ever get back to its original meaning?

The vogue for fiction is tremendous now, even in the children's field. Many publishers publish nothing else. Many editors would not consider a manuscript that was not fictional. Many authors prefer to write fiction. Perhaps it is quicker and easier to make up an improbable story than to go out to life and get a real one. In fiction, anything can happen. You are not bound by any rules or regulations, although, strangely enough, fiction has taken on stereotyped formulas and patterns both in character-portrayal and plot-construction, which shows that the imagination has definite limitations.

In writing of real life, an author is bound and restricted by many things—by the laws of nature and human nature, by the unpredictability of human behavior, by conditioning factors of occupation and environment, and by the quirks of human character. In real life, people do not behave in a fictional manner. People do not conform to set fictional patterns. They are too "ornery" for that!

Real people are not always consistent, for instance. They do not always perform "in character." One person is not all white and the next all black; we are all varying shades of gray. One is not all good and another all evil. Most of us are somewhere in between. A peace-loving person may sometimes quarrel. A lover of animals might even kill one.

So whenever an author says, "What *would* a character do in such a situation?" and relies on his own imagination to answer the question, he is on very dangerous ground. People do not behave the way we think they might or even the way they are supposed to behave. Human nature is unending in its variety and pattern. The motives behind human behavior are devious, never set and formalized, always flexible and ever-changing. It is better to ask: "What *did* they do in this situation, and *why* did they do it?" rather than: "What would they do?" or "What do I think they ought to do, or should do?"

My experience in writing real-life stories has taught me one thing—human behavior is not fictional. I no longer use the conventional ruses and devices of fiction to build my stories. The only rules I follow are the rules of living observed in others. I do not superimpose artificial, synthetic plots upon my real-life characters. My plots grow out of the happenings of daily life. Human life in its basic essence needs no glamorization or exaggeration. It has all the elements of vital drama inherent in itself.

In real life, a child's character can grow and develop, it can be shaped and changed by circumstances and by human relations. A book can show those things that influence a child's character for better or for worse. A book can tell of a child's adjustment to a new environment, of his homesickness for his former home; of a child's adjustment to a parent's misfortune or to a physical handicap. All these can be worthy themes for a child's book. Such themes, I admit, are not as exciting and glamorous as paying off the family mortgage, going to the moon, solving mysteries like professional detectives or discovering secret gold mines. But synthetic excitement and glamour and false values are not the goals we are seeking for our boys and girls, when we urge them to read books.

What are the benefits from books which have their source in real life? Why should children read them?

Books of this type are a two-way street. They take from life, and they give back to life. Even as they grow out of life, they confirm and extend life.

The imaginative book satisfies and delights a child at certain stages and in certain moods. They appeal to his sense of humor and his love of the impossible. No child should be without them. But fictional stories do not satisfy a child's curiosity about living. They cannot for they deal with preposterous situations that have no relation to living. The people portrayed are cardboard characters who have never lived nor breathed. The plots are artificial and implausible. The hero's selfish desire to get what he wants is always gratified.

The most dangerous thing about fiction, however, is that it too often masquerades as real life. The child reader swallows it whole and believes it, to his own undoing. Even when he questions it, wondering, "Is this true or not?" how is he to be sure? Floundering and bewildered, his confidence in books in shattered. Why should he go on reading? When fiction is confused with reality, it becomes doubly harmful. If children cannot recognize truth when they see it, then something is wrong with the books they are reading.

By way of contrast, what does the honest real-life story offer? Books that grow out of life not only confirm and nourish life, but they extend life as well.

Children are true realists. Even in their imaginative play, do they make up fantastic creatures that never existed? No, only adults do that. Children play lady, nurse, teacher, mother, doctor, truck-driver, cowboy, robber, aviator, policeman. They re-enact dramas of real life—they cook, eat and sleep, they give medicine to sick dolls, they preach funeral sermons and bury dead birds, they ride horses and rope cows. They re-enact scenes from real life so seriously they seem to be rehearsing for the adult stage of life far in the future. Their imagination always has its roots in the ground.

The great advantage of the true-to-life book, therefore, is that it touches children's own lives. The best reaction from a book, shared with a group, is self-identification. A child interrupts and says, "I did that. I caught a baby bird once." Or, "Our cow had a calf out in the pasture too." Or, "I got lost one time and could not find the way home"—just like the child in the book. Group reading of a book should bring out a chorus of responses, in which the children compare the book experiences with their own. When a dog appears, every child wants to tell about his own dog and compare it with the dog in the book. Often children draw valuable deductions and apply the moral to their own conduct.

I had a letter from a teacher of remedial reading in Miami, Florida. She told of a big strapping ninth grade boy who was reading at third grade level. All her efforts to interest him in reading failed until he happened on a copy of *Peanuts for Billy Ben*. "*We* call 'em *goobers!*" he cried in excitement. He asked to take the book home with him. The next day, he inquired: "You ain't got nary 'nother book just like this one, have you?" His interest in reading had been aroused. After some months, he was reading at seventh grade level, and became an active member of the school's Teen-age Book Club. Goobers and peanuts meant something in that boy's life and served as a bridge to take him into the world of literature.

My books about the way children live in the South have, I believe, served two purposes. Not only have they extended life for our northern, urban, middle-class children, by showing them that a real world exists completely unlike but just as real as their own, and by helping them to share it vicariously, but these books have touched the lives of thousands of southern children, who never knew that books could be about themselves. For the first time they have identified themselves in books. "We never picked cotton in a book before!" cried the children of Arkansas.

Reading of familiar things and identifying oneself with them is but a step to further growth. Self-identification leads the child away from himself on an unfamiliar path into the unknown, into the world of other people. It leads him to vicarious identification. How is he able to project himself into the personality of strangers and share their experiences as if they happened to himself? The real understanding of anyone else, be it a child or an adult, people different from ourselves, or nations different from our own, can be accomplished in only one way, by putting ourselves in the other person's place, by vicarious identification.

To put ourselves in the other person's place is to think as he thinks. It is a very grave error to ascribe to others our own aspirations and desires. Other people do not necessarily think as we do. Can we put ourselves into their thoughts and think as they think? What we must feel for them is not so much sympathy, but empathy—a total identification with the other person's feelings and situation. We are too prone to see people, not as *they* are, but as *we* are.

In Burma, it did no good for the technical assistance experts to show the inhabitants how to grow tomatoes and to talk about this healthful addition to their diet. The Burmese people do not eat tomatoes. In Venezuela, the housewives refused to abolish their colorful open-air markets and to have them replaced by indoor American supermarkets. The outdoor market was their way of life. In Africa, a modern village was deserted because the builders put running water into all the houses. The women rebelled, because their only excuse for social contact with their own kind at the village well had been taken away from them. So we must try to forget our own thinking, to think as they think, and to project ourselves into their feelings and situation. After self-identification, we move onward to vicarious identification with others.

Human experience is so limited, it can be greatly broadened by reading books. In fact, this is about the only way that children, or adults, can get a vivid glimpse into the inner life and thought-processes of a strange person—by sharing it in a book. This is made possible because the author has gone direct to real people for his story, and by his gifts of creation and imagination, has laid bare the strange person's thoughts, emotions, motives and intentions.

Real life, everyday life is important. It is endlessly rich in substance and meaning. A great novelist has said: "Anything that happens on any one day to any one man is important." Carlyle once said that if a man had seeing eyes he could view life in its entirety in a tiny roadside village as fully as if he were to travel round the world. All synthetic plots are pallid beside the miraculous richness of daily life.

What kind of response should we get from children to real-life stories which present an alien environment? Group sharing of a book should arouse spontaneous discussions on moral and ethical implications. Such discussions are evidence that the book has made the children think. They are of far more value than the writing of book reviews or book reports. One child's candid reaction will stir the others to similar or contrary points of view. If an argument ensues, all the better!

Often, children need help when exploring a world unfamiliar to them. Sometimes their reactions are negative, based on a smug satisfaction with their own way of life, which is so narrow they cannot bridge the chasm to a broader experience. A child reading *Blue Ridge Billy* said: "I wouldn't like it if I had to carry water from a spring. I'd rather turn on the tap!" A boy reading *Judy's Journey* said: "I'm glad my daddy has a steady job and a good salary." A group of children in Michigan wrote me: "We laughed and laughed over the way they talked in *Strawberry Girl.*" Such negative reactions indicate a lack of guidance on the part of the leader. The real meaning of the book was lost on the children, who were so deeply absorbed in their own concerns, they were unable to forget them.

Let me give some examples of thoughtful reactions:

When a group of Wisconsin children read *Cotton in My Sack,* they became greatly concerned for the plight of the cotton farmer and his family, and had these constructive suggestions to make: "I think they ought to rotate crops and not plant just cotton." "Why can't the owner give them work to do in the winter-time, maybe in the cotton-gin?" "Do the cotton people go to church on Sunday? Oh, I hope they do!" After a tornado struck a town in eastern Indiana, the children there voluntarily asked to re-read the storm chapters in *Judy's Journey* and *Boom-Town Boy,* to compare the storms described with their own rugged experiences. They came to a new appreciation of *Blue Ridge Billy* as well. With electricity cut off for two weeks, they had to carry water in pails just like the mountain children.

And so a book becomes a door, an open door to wider understanding. It helps a child to see beyond his own life into the lives of others. And when it takes him inside the hero's heart and mind, he finds he has found a brother.

Yes, books are to be greatly treasured. They take from life and they give back to life. Even as they grow out of life, they are all-embracing—they extend our compassion and reverence for all living things.

Otherness

THE TRAVELER

There's a hard road to travel
and you don't go by car;
From your mind to my mind
the distance is far.
From my heart to your heart
how can I go?
By love and kindness—
the only road I know.

There's a hard road to travel
and you don't go by plane;
From your world to my world,
a long winding lane.
In my life and your life,
what can we share?
Friendship and kindness—
if we put it there.

SOCIAL LIVING is living with other people. John Donne, the poet, said, "No man is an island," meaning that no man can live to himself alone. Social living means relationships—with your family, parents, brothers and sisters, relatives; with your neighbors and your community; with strangers; with your country and the world. It means relationships with people in all these areas.

Education is now facing many problems and demands—juvenile deportment, character development, the restoration of spiritual values and the creation of world-mindedness. Beneath all these is the basic problem of helping children to understand others. The schools sometimes make gestures in this direction. They may put on an assembly program on UNESCO, or a movie on juvenile delinquency, or lectures on basic virtues or provide books on the great religions. More, much more needs to be done if we are to teach children how to live.

In 1899 William James, the great psychologist and philosopher, gave a lecture to teachers, entitled, "Of a Certain Blindness." The blindness in human beings of which he spoke is the blindness with which we are all afflicted in regard to the feelings of others. In his life and in all his writings, William James tried to dispel that blindness. He stressed the acquiring of a sense of *otherness.*

This blindness is self-centered. It can be easily seen in our usual attitude to our neighbor. *My* pain is intense—*his* is light. *My* feelings are deep—*his* are callous, indifferent or dull. *I* am a person—*he* is a clod. *I* am generous—*he* is selfish. To overcome this blindness, to acquire a sense of otherness and a vision of true understanding, should be the goal of all education.

Modern education in its zeal for imparting facts and information and for teaching skills should develop an equal concern over the right attitudes for applying this knowledge and these skills. Too much of the knowledge gained from books tends to be generalized, overlooks the human approach, deals with facts and information, forgetting the basic commodity beneath everything—people. We must translate facts and figures into human terms, we must extend our experience, deepen our insight, learn to dispel the blindness of egotism and acquire a sense of true otherness.

The first step is developing a curiosity and interest in other people, in how they live and why. Our world has become very small, due to the ease of transportation by auto and airplane, the mass production and distribution of food and all supplies, and mass means of communication. These things have brought people closer together. Whether we like it or not, people different from ourselves have moved into our consciousness and into our daily lives. Industry and labor and economics are shifting families of all classes from one part of the country to another. America, since the days of the ox-cart and the covered wagon, is more on the move than ever. *Anybody* can become your next-door neighbor or fellow-worker.

What are you going to do about it? There is only one answer. Try to understand him. Try to put yourself in his place and see what his problems are. We must learn more about the beliefs and customs of our neighbors, about their methods of work, their cultural backgrounds, their hopes and ideals, their problems and trials, so we can better understand their actions, their habits and their attitudes.

Sir Wilfred Grenfell said: "The world is slowly learning that because two men think differently, neither need be wicked." We must make allowances for the amazing variety in mankind, and thank God we are not all alike on the outside. Our curiosity about our neighbor and his ways will always be sympathetic and constructive instead of critical and destructive, once we learn a sense of true otherness.

The second step is learning to bridge the gap of differences. When we try to understand the other person, we have to span the barriers that keep us apart. There are many such barriers—of social position and intellect, of language and dialect—people don't always talk as we do—of cleanliness, of culture, of dress, of race, color and religion. Surely in God's eyes these differences must be infinitesimal, but in man's eyes, they often assume gigantic proportions.

We must recognize the presence in the world of people we do not like, people in another social or economic class lower than our own, people whose habits and customs are not like ours, people rough, uncouth, lacking in manners, even those who are weak, spineless, low, wicked, vicious, criminal. Ignoring these people, pretending they do not exist, is not helping them. Our attitude and concern should be: What made them that way? Were their homes wrong? Parents wrong? Environment bad? How can I be tolerant of such people and live in the same world with them? How can I help them? Help children to avoid a similar fate?

It is not enough to stay safe in one's own little corner, smugly satisfied with one's own life. After awareness comes concern, an active concern about others, a constant striving to be of service, to make the world a better place for children, and, for teachers, to make up to children for all the lacks in their lives. To offset the differences, we look for likenesses and it is amazing how many we can find. All people alike share a love of family and children, the need for friendship and love, a desire for security and for an adequate means of livelihood, a need to worship God and a love of the beautiful.

How can we get close to a stranger? To an enemy?

Find some common denominator and use it. There is always one, though it may be hidden. Perhaps there is a common interest—a love of flowers, of dogs, of games, or a common ailment and common cures. I've got rheumatism too. What do you do for yours? Or an interest in food and recipes. How do you cook eggplant? I fry mine in lard! Or jobs and occupations, ways of working, or similar recreations. It can be any one of a hundred things to bind two people together.

For three years until she died, I had a fine relationship with Mama Hattie, a character in one of my Regional books. Although I had a college education and she went only to the third grade, although I am white and she was black, although I have much and she had little, although I lived in a good house and she in a shack, we found we had much in common, as we compared our respective ways of life and the problems of living. She used to say: "I never went to school, but I've got mother-wit to bring up my children."

She had an instinctive wisdom that I held in high regard, and her passing left an emptiness in my heart and life.

There is always a meeting place of minds and hearts, if we take the time and trouble to look for it. True otherness, true tolerance, is the disposition to enjoy, or at least to suffer patiently, the idiosyncracies of others which are dissimilar to our own. It is a willingness to embrace within our world lives with which one could not pretend to sympathize, but which are admirable on their own terms, however unintelligible to us. William James felt that otherness should not be reluctantly conceded or bravely endured, but welcomed with a glad heart. Are any of us big enough in heart and soul to do this?

What we can do is learn to make allowances. You never know what is behind a questionable action. You never know, judging only from the surface, the pain and trouble in the lives of others. You never know what is behind the emotional behavior of a difficult child. Pain and trouble are usually buried deep under layers of camouflage.

The third step in understanding others is identification. We must change places with others and stand in their shoes. To understand others, we must relate their problems to our own. In facing up to their problems and difficulties through personal sharing or through the reading of an honest book, we can come closer. We can learn what it means to live in blighted areas, to be confined in certain social, economic and religious brackets, to be judged by outward circumstances rather than by inner worth, to be judged by hasty action rather than by serious intent.

To gain a sense of otherness is a process in self-education. Tolstoi, writing of the Russian peasant, said: "I had to love these people. The more I entered into their life, the more I loved them; and the more it became possible for *me* to *live* too." A Chinese proverb says: "Be not disturbed at being misunderstood; be disturbed rather at not being understanding." True democracy and true religion begin in the hearts of men.

And so otherness becomes a boomerang. It reverts back on oneself with astonishing force. The habit of searching out the best in people enlarges our own souls. William James vividly describes this experience: "The scales seemed to fall from my eyes; and a wave of sympathy greater than anything I had ever before felt with the life of common man began to fill my soul."

I had a similar experience. While working with the cotton children in Arkansas, I grew so close to them through the poignant stories they told me of their lives, I was engulfed in compassion. I felt I had to tell their story which had never been told before. I forgot myself and my own life as I lived with them, and when it was time to go, the parting was difficult, on both sides.

Otherness enriches the soul of him who possesses it. He will never be the same again. As William James said, "To live generously and lovingly is a profound experience."

If you were the wisest man in the world and could have but one wish granted you, what would you pray for? Peace? Power? Long life? Wealth? Learning? This question is not hypothetical. When it was asked of King Solomon, he answered that he wanted none of these things. Instead, if there was but one thing he could have, he asked to be able to tell the difference between good and evil. He asked for an understanding heart.

Hints to Young Writers

LIVING

A baby's cry
A woman's soft word;
Children playing –
The song of a bird.

A house with a porch
A letter in the mail;
The ring of the phone,
A girl with a pail.

A seed in the earth,
The green leaves grow;
Living is growing –
Yearning to know.

THE BEGINNING writer always asks: What can I write about? The professor of creative writing will tell him, "Write about what you know." The student will say, "My own life is stupid and dull." That, of course, is the time to study the lives of other people.

How do you do it, I am often asked. How do you go among strangers and find out how they live? My own approach has been made easy by the fact that I am an artist. When I sit sketching on a street corner or in a grocery store on a village street, people become curious and ask questions. After a while, I ask them questions about their interests, their occupations, their crops, their problems. They know more about themselves than I do, and are glad to answer.

Even if you are not an artist, when going for a motor trip in a new part of the country, it is easy to stop and talk to people working in a field or to the men coming from a factory or to women in a department store. Ask them about all those things they know so much better than you. Win their confidence. If a farmer's crop has failed, he'll be glad to tell you why. If you show your ignorance about the workings of a coal mine, a miner will be glad to enlighten you. If you see such people frequently, show a kindly sympathy and interest, you will get to know more and more about them. Most people are good story-tellers and like to tell of their childhood or of everyday experiences, if given a sympathetic listener. Ride a bus and talk to your seat-mate. A few questions will open up a vivid glimpse of this stranger's life.

A wealth of stories is available from older people in all our regions, from people who like to reminisce of their past and interpret the present. Our novelists have greatly neglected this field. Children, too, can tell wonderful stories of their experiences. The average twelve-year-old boy is an excellent informant, for he knows as much or more than his father about his father's business or occupation. He has a tremendous store of information on scientific, agricultural and general subjects. In many environments, the twelve-year-old boy is amazingly adult, independent, reliable and trustworthy. When I want to know things, accurate details that other people omit, I go to the twelve-year-old boy!

In spite of our mass communications and increasing standardization, we are still not all alike, we do not all think or act alike, for our lives are governed by our occupations and by the environment itself. There are many outward differences that keep us divided, that keep us from understanding each other. I have felt that there is a real need for books which make clear that people are what they are due to forces often beyond their control and, for this reason, they deserve all our love and understanding. Through such books, we are able to come closer to them in true brotherhood.

So I suggest to you who want to write, are trying to write or hope to write, that you forget yourself, forget this precious self of yours that you have been told to express, forget this undeveloped self which has had so little experience and knows so little. Get out of yourself and project yourself into the lives of others. Get out of your ivory tower, get out of the safe, protected campus world, if you are a college student, and become interested in other people and their concerns. Project yourself into their problems with sympathetic understanding to find out how they live, what they think and say and do, what their joys and sorrows are, what their goals and ambitions are, or what it is that keeps them from having goals and ambitions, if they have none. Once you bury yourself in their concerns, you will find you have something to write about.

In other words, you must first enrich your own soul, if you expect to give anything to others.

Now, about actual methods. If you have gone out into the world of people and things, you will automatically have filled pages and pages of a large fat notebook with notes; notes of fleeting personal impressions—the ominous look of the sky on a stormy day, the fragile smile on the dirty face of a child, the feeling of desolation that stabs you in an underprivileged home, the gayety of elation shared with a boy in a moment of triumph, the tone of despair in a sad mother's voice. Things like these—momentary impressions that hit you hard and make a deep impact—jot them down in words.

Soon your notebook will be jammed with personal experiences, not yours but of others—anecdotes and tales of all kinds from young and old, tales an old man tells of his boyhood, stories of what happened just yesterday to a boy or girl in the nearest school or met on the street corner, factual details told by men, who are apt to leave out the human side of living, whether from shyness, indifference or distrust, I do not know; the best stories of all coming to you from women, young or old, women who more than men, seem to sense the meaning of life and who are willing to share it with you. Not all will be willing, some will confront you with closed lips, but for all unwilling, there are a hundred who will be generous and responsive. For many, it will be an outlet greatly needed and well deserved.

In this way, your notebook will soon be chockful of real experiences, simple things that have happened to real people in everyday life, not dramatic historical events glamorized by the passing of years, not fantastic made-up adventures which you try to evoke out of a feeble, ineffective imagination. But simple things that make up the heart of everyday living—a woman at a mail-box, reading a letter from her long-lost son, a child digging in the earth to plant a few seeds, a mother hanging clothes on the line, a father coming home with lunch pail in his hand. These are the simple dramas of which real life is made.

You will have pages and pages of speech notations too. In no two regions of our country do people speak alike. The use of words is a definite key to character. The people in your book are to speak as people in real life speak, not the way you yourself speak, not the way English grammar tells us to speak, for speech is a living thing, taking on the character of the speaker. A close observation and study of the rhythms of American speech is a good thing, not only for the poet, but also for the prose writer.

Your notebook will be crammed with visual images of all kinds. If, like me, you are an artist, there will be many pages of drawings to refer to later. But even an artist may not have the time or opportunity to make a drawing—things happen too fast—when you enter a strange home for the first time. And so you store impressions in your memory. With great and sensitive awareness, you look around, see and sense and feel your surroundings and take away stored images in your mind, images etched sometimes in acid so deep they can never be erased. If you come from the average or better than average American home, it will be a revelation and an education to you to enter a sharecropper's home, a poor Negro's cabin in the colored quarter of a town, a slum apartment in your own city, a river fisherman's houseboat or a tarpaper migrant shanty.

Go—go to some of these places on your summer vacation, and volunteer your services to help. Look around you with love and sympathy, talk to a child in a cotton field pulling a nine-foot sack, or to a sick mother on a pallet bed in a tumble-down shack or to her husband out of work. Study the faces of passers-by on a busy city street, and try to imagine what made them that way. Train yourself to see character behind the human mask.

Store your mind with visual images, store your heart with human stories of the way that other people live. Then come back home and write. You will find you have something to write about. The hardest part will be the problem of selection —from that richly-crammed notebook of yours.

If you have truly lived in this world of people and things, you will have no trouble. Your story will write itself. You will not be afraid to put real people into your book, with changed names of course. You might start by writing a biographical sketch of one of the story-tellers you have listened to, then of another whose life was intertwined with the first. That is a good beginning.

Listen to the problems of the people you meet and find out how they solved them or failed to do so. Listen to their conflicts. Did they win or lose? And why? There you have a plot—conflicting forces working against each other. Of course, real life does not solve its plots as neatly and happily as fiction does. So you will have a conflict of your own, to decide what the solution shall be—whether to be faithful to truth or to cater to wishful thinking. After your major conflict is decided upon, you may want to make an outline, jotting down progressive steps toward the solution, gradually enriching it with all the minor side-plots you wish to include, until a chapter by chapter outline is complete.

Only then are you ready to write. The success of your story will depend upon the amount of preparation, the amount of dedication you have given. You must first enrich your own soul if you expect to have anything to give. Writing a book is giving to your readers your interpretation of life as you see it. Cramming that notebook of yours is also a process of cramming your heart and mind with good things, with rich insights and deep understanding.

Once you do this, you need no longer worry about your imagination, or your sub-conscious, you need only to write, and you will have something to say that people will want to read, that people will want to hear. May all the joy of creative writing be yours!

Look at the Child

I AM WHAT I DO

I am play
I am flight
I am work
I am fright.

I am bread
I am milk
I am cotton
and silk.

I am hope
I am fears
I am love
I am tears.

I am smiles
so bright
I am joy
and delight.

JUST HOW DOES an author write a book?

I wish I could give you a simple recipe, as for baking a cake. It might run something like this: One cup of information, one cup of excitement, one-half cup plot, one-half cup danger, three tablespoons imagination plus a sprinkling of humor and a dash of nonsense. Shake well in an electric mixer and out comes a book! Oh yes, I forgot—add one rattlesnake! I shall always remember the serious little girl who once told me that "A good book always has a rattlesnake in it!"

But alas! a book is not written that way. Writing a book is an intangible process, in which an author has mostly only his own instinct and insight to guide him. The books on HOW TO WRITE JUVENILES do not help him. He pays no attention to educational jargon and gobbledygook. He doesn't even know the meaning of phrases like "reading readiness," "developmental growth," "emotional attitudes," "comprehension and frustration levels" and the like. His surest guide is his own instinct and insight and this is (and always should be) backed up by a basic understanding of children, the kind that can only come with constant observation and close rapport with children.

There are many ways to write books, for writing is always a very personal matter. Some books for children are dashed off in a frenzy of excitement or imagination, some are pulled, like aching teeth, out of his consciousness and laboriously and painfully put down on paper, with hundreds of changes and erasures. Some are casual memories of childhood told by a doting grandmother or uncle, others are fantastic efforts to be cute or funny or outrageous, by people who like to exploit children.

But most of our best books are not written in any of these ways. To most of us, the writing of a book for children is not a slight or a casual thing, but the result of a constant awareness, of lifelong observation and study and of a continuous devotion to our task. I think we never feel sure enough of ourselves to say just how we do it, or how the children help us—for without their help, our books could not come into being.

When I say that we are, perhaps, blessed with an instinctive understanding of children, which is probably what makes us an author in the first place, I say it in all humility. The true lovers of children are always humble before the marvels of childhood and awed by its potentialities. Even as children grow and change, so must our ideas of guidance and interpretation grow and change.

Rousseau, the great educator, said: "Look at the child and see what he is like." And so we look—with an open and inquiring mind, and the more we learn, the more there is to learn. There are no final answers. I suppose it is true that of all the various fields of education, ideas regarding the education and training of children have gone through more different phases than that of any other group. New trends are constantly disputing and disregarding previous ones only lately held sacrosanct. We are all trying to learn what is best for the child, changing our ideas and coming up with new ones, discarding the old. This very process shows that while we have the child and his welfare close at heart, no one, least of all ourselves, ever knows the answer. So we keep on with the search, following the motto: "Look at the child and see what he is like."

For my own books, this is not only symbolically but literally true. Without the inspiration and help of children, they could not have been written. Many of them have grown out of actual contacts with children. All have grown out of whatever understanding I have acquired through years of reflective observation and association with children.

For my picture books I choose all my own subjects, usually submitting a dummy of drawings with a tentative text, to present the idea. At this stage the book is shown to children of the age for which it is intended and I listen to their candid comments, making changes accordingly, for I have the highest regard for their opinions and judgments. Their comments and questions often show me what is wrong with my original version. Then, after I receive the editor's approval, I rework the drawings and text into finished form.

I must add that my editors are always kind and ask for a minimum of changes. In fact, they have spoiled me completely for they give me my own way most of the time.

My main work comes, however, long before presentation to the editor, while working on the idea. Some ideas are in the making as long as ten years before they can be put on paper. They might be inspired by a single phrase spoken by a child or a single incident observed or by a series of happenings. Or they might grow out of the whole basic body of knowledge that children have given me over the years.

One child alone can provide material for many books. The Mr. Small books grew out of my observation of the play of my four-year-old son, Stephen, and his playmates. In a single summer which he spent with me, Davy, my step-daughter's three-year-old, inspired six pre-school picture books, later called the Davy books. Even so, even though the ideas come from children, adult concepts have a way of creeping in. For this reason, I always feel the necessity of taking each book in dummy form to children and studying their reactions. Once I face a group, often even before I have read the story aloud or shown them the rough sketches for the pictures, I instinctively sense what is wrong. Their very presence helps me to see and feel it, even before they ask questions or say a word.

My Regional and Roundabout America books have also grown from association with children who live in the different regions of our country. These children have in many instances invited me to come, and have always voluntarily taken me into their schools, homes and daily lives, sharing every detail. They have shared not only their happiness with me but their problems and trials as well, giving me an all-round picture of their way of life. All their contributions have added richly to the sum-total of my story.

"Look at the child and see what he is like," has ever been my motto and guiding principle in seeking to know the different children I have met in our regions. Each is unique and different. One can only understand them by taking a long and serious and loving look.

These "middle-age" children have been of immeasurable help, too, in judging my stories while still in manuscript, before publication. They have helped to point out inconsistencies, or a lack of clarity. They have helped in judging the story by their own experience, so different from the children in the story, and in relating and contrasting the two environments. Their comments and suggestions help me to present the story in such a way that my readers may bridge the gap from their own limited experience to the wider experience of understanding others.

Creating Books

ROOTS

What is this power that pulls me
Unresisting, limp, leading me on?
What is this compelling urge that draws me
As a bending flower is lifted to the sun?

This oneness with a place,
This identity of self with face,
This kinship makes us one.

The succulent shoots and fond tendrils
hold me fast,
My roots have grown down too deeply
for me to cut them off.

These are my people
and this is my country
where I belong.

CREATING BOOKS for children has been the joy of my life. It has been my pleasure and privilege to write and illustrate books for children from the ages of one and a half to fourteen, in various age groups. I have never tired of it. Each creation has been a joy and a delight.

It all began many years ago, when I was living a very isolated life in a remote part of New England, and when I felt very much cut off from the world. My son was growing up and so I began making picture books for him. Older and longer stories followed. One by one, from that isolated little studio on the edge of a hayfield, my books went out into the world, making friends for me all over the country. In such a way, when I least suspected it, I can see now that I was following the path of my destiny. A little later, an opportunity came for travel back and forth across the United States, and so a new world opened up for me, not only for the widening of my own personal experience but providing a never-ending source of material for my books.

I was given the privilege of sharing in the lives of children in many different environments and to show, through my stories, how American children live. Our children are not all alike, they do not all think, speak and act alike, they are products of that little piece of our country in which their roots happen to have been put down, in which they grow and flourish or, as sometimes happens, survive against adversity.

I have learned a high regard for children. No matter where he lives, the child retains his capacity for astonishment and wonder, his eager curiosity about life and all those indefinable sensations that the impact of his own little world makes upon him. He may not understand the stereotyped conformist world we usually consider our American way of life, but he knows and understands every detail of his own small world. I never fail to be amazed at children's versatility. They are wise and thoughtful, often stoical, meeting whatever comes with resilience and equanimity, yet always retaining an innate capacity for sensing the joy of life. And yet it is wrong to make generalizations about them. Each child is an individual, each a person in his own right, and what he is is determined largely by the place where he lives.

Come with me. Let us look at the ways of life in our country. Let us go into out-of-the-way corners, up on the hills and down in the valleys, into city streets and village homes. Let us see and get to know the children. Here and there, roundabout America, are friends worth knowing.

Come with me. I will take the reader by the hand and together we will go into a mountain cabin, a snowbound schoolhouse out on the prairie, a floating houseboat on the Mississippi River, a barracks housing project in a large city.

Come with me. Down on the bayou in Louisiana, a little girl called Suzette is fishing. She takes her string of fish to Pere Eugene, the country storekeeper, and swaps them for groceries, plus a little tobacco for Papa Jules, who cannot work because he has a bullet in his back. Out in the middle of a cotton field in Arkansas, Joanda is pulling a nine-foot sack full of cotton. She tells me a poignant story, how her brother Ricky was run over by the boss-man's tractor and all the trouble that it made. There's a brand-new tractor on the corn farm in Iowa, and Dick, even if he has rheumatic fever, is determined to drive it—until he has a bad spill.

Up on the mountains in the Blue Ridge, a boy sits on a rail fence, watching the sun go down. He is worried about the moonshiners hidden away in the underbrush, and about the trouble that threatens Granny Trivett in her cabin near the big cowcumber tree. Padding along on her bare feet in the white sand behind the old white mule, Birdie Boyer feels the hot Florida sun beating down upon her head and wonders how contemptible her neighbors can be. Out in South Dakota a blizzard is raging, and a brother and sister are trying to make their way through waist-high drifts to get home from school. Should they have stayed all night and slept on the hard school floor as Teacher wanted them to do? Or will they be able to get home safely?

In an old half-broken jalopy, Judy in overalls

rides along singing, *You are my Sunshine,* happy although she has no idea where she will sleep that night or what she will have to eat for the next meal. A big passenger train chugs along the railroad track, and a little dark-skinned girl thinks longingly of the beloved grandmother she has left behind and is fearful of the changes that city life will bring.

In the middle of the Mississippi river, a little girl lives on an island, and when the johnboat has gone up or down river, she has no way to cross over to the mainland or to call the doctor when illness strikes. A boy on a peanut farm in eastern North Carolina works like a man to help get the crop out. Another boy in a northern city has his home in a two-room barracks housing project on a city dump, and there he runs and plays. On a Texas ranch, a girl maliciously gallops her pony across her neighbor's vegetable patch, and a boy in Oklahoma lives through the excitement of the coming of oil on his father's farm.

These are real children, everyday American children. These are all real children I have known and loved, whom I have visited and who have taken me into their hearts and homes and lives.

These are children I have written about. They are not dream children, whom I have imagined. They are all flesh and blood. As I tell you about each in turn, and the setting in which he lives, I can visualize clearly the living child I had the privilege to know. I use the present rather than the past tense, for although many of them have grown to manhood and womanhood since I knew them, they are still alive, as children, in my books.

How does one write a book? The creative process is difficult to put into words. It is not easy to explain how an author puts a real child on the printed page, so that the child and his experiences will come alive for the reader.

The first step is preparation.

The mind must first be filled, saturated to the point of overflowing, with the subject matter. It must be so filled with it, that all other considerations are crowded out, that one's daily life becomes routine and puppet-like—so real is the life being lived within the mind. This can only be possible when the author has, through the closest kind of association with the people she wants to write about, forgetting her own life and her very existence, identified herself with them in all sympathy and understanding.

When such, almost sacred, preparation has been made, then one is ready to proceed. Not only the conscious but the unconscious mind is ready to help. By some remarkable process, which probably only our Divine Creator can explain, the story takes form, an outline appears, and scene by scene, the story unrolls like a panorama, with little conscious control. Somehow this elusive material, the fragile breath of the great adventure of living, resolves itself into the form and shape of a book, notwithstanding all the many tangible requirements of plot, style, format, line, page, chapter and manuscript length. To take this living material and compress it into the mold of the printed word is not easy.

To make and place in the pages at strategic points, illustrations which not only interpret but enrich and amplify the drama, is also no simple task. I have often felt that not I but some greater power was guiding my pencil, enabling me to put intangible qualities into a drawing, qualities that my conscious mind had not conceived at all. By some strange alchemy, places seen with human eyes, adventures humorous, tragic or commonplace heard with human ears, elusive thoughts, feelings and emotions experienced by a group of people somehow fuse themselves together into one artistic whole, assuming all the requirements of bookmaking and become that wonderful creation—a book. After such experiences, it is easy to believe that the making of a book is truly a creative process.

I live with the people I want to write about *before* I write about them. I live with them in spirit *while* I am writing about them. I see them alive before me as I put their likenesses down on paper in the form of words and illustrations.

I do not live in an ivory tower, apart from the world, and dream up my characters. I could not dream them up because the human imagination is inadequate. I could never imagine children like those I have described to you. Many children's books do have imaginary characters and plots concocted in the mind of the author. There is a limit to human inventiveness, and such plots are apt to become repetitious, the resulting theme to be one of selfishness—the hero wanting something, and after certain frustrating obstacles are removed, getting it.

Real life is not so neat. The plots of real life are not found in the "How to be a Successful Author" book. The plots of real life are not fantastic things, masquerading, condoned and often praised as imaginative—things like finding treasure in a hidden cave, exposing the bad guys and getting them arrested or even paying off the mortgage. Real children do not do things like this. Why not put real children into books?

No—the plots of real life are not so flashy; they are more subtle. They are perhaps, the drama of siblings and playmates, the drama of growing up, the drama of the adjustment to a new situation or change of environment, the mastering of fear by the acquisition of courage, the hazardous drama of a parent's occupation, always so deeply felt by a child. Real life needs no apologies. It is full of drama, which needs no artificial manufacturing. Things like these have to be seen through a child's eye and mind first, before the depth of their interpretation can be achieved in the pages of a book.

How can an author share the lives of others?

All creative work is based on feeling.

An artist or an author (to me, they are one and the same) has to *feel* what he does. To draw the picture of a child sweeping with a broom, I myself must first take broom in hand and go through the motions of sweeping. To draw a boy pumping an old-fashioned pump, I have to leave my desk, pump a pump in pantomime, then go back to my desk and amazingly, I find I can draw it! To draw a child picking cotton, and to write convincingly about it, I must first go into the cotton field with the children and pick cotton with them. I have to bend my back, feel long hours of hot sunshine upon my shoulders, endure the weariness of the never-ending day—only then can I share the cotton child's life well enough to write of it.

Even in a picture book for the pre-school child, I, as author and artist, must somehow catch up the essence of the small child's world, forget my adult world and way of thinking, become a child at heart, live with him his simple doings and activity, listen to his every word with respect, and try to interpret all he does. To the very young child, a drawing is not a picture on paper, a convention in two dimensions; it is a real happening. When the three-year-old sees the boy in the picture holding a boat in his hand, he says to him, "Put it down. Put the boat in the water!" The picture boat, boy and water are as real to him as reality itself. And so the author-artist must sense this, and draw pictures that have the very breath of life in them.

To write the Roundabout and Regional stories, it was not enough to do research in the library and *read about* a particular region. Even a single week spent in the region itself is worth six weeks spent in the library. Why? Because all the things I want to know about people and the way they live have been left out of the books, and only the surface, the outward things, the superficialities, kept in. I do not want hearsay, I do not want the opinions of others on the way they *think* these people live. I want to talk to them myself, to hear their tone of voice, to hear the way they pronounce their words, to see the pain or the joy in their eyes, to listen to the child's outpourings myself. I want to become one with the people who live in the region.

That is why I must go there. The hardest of all journeys is into the heart and mind of another person. We seldom know those who live with us, whom we see and talk to daily. To share an alien way of life means first forgetting oneself completely, only then can I take on the new and different and make it my own. Just how it is done, how one gets beneath the skin, how one learns to share the mind and heart of another is a creative process I cannot explain. All I know is that it is necessary. While I was born in Ohio and lived there in my growing years, and since then have lived for thirty years in New England, my home place is elsewhere. My roots have been put down in each of the regions I have written about. I have not one, but many home places. Something of my heart is left in each place that I write about.

One can tell only the outward things. Days spent talking to children and listening, always listening, visiting their school, their homes, getting to know their parents and earning their confidence, eating at the kitchen table in the heart of the family. A definite identification with each child chosen as hero or heroine, many days and weeks of thinking as he thinks, doing as he does, re-living with him all the dramatic moments which he so trustingly and candidly and often poignantly confides—often things he would not tell his own parents—all these things help make the child come alive in word and picture. And so my books become a mirror held up to life, to reflect back all its reality, not a distorted picture all "sweetness and light," but its flaws and sadness as well as its joys and its beauties.

To write of real children means a close rapport with them, a positive identification with them. I must *be* that child in spirit for many months while the work is in progress. I eat, sleep, speak and act as the child acts. He becomes more real to me than members of my own family whom I am seeing daily, because I have entered his mind and thought. I think and feel as he thinks and feels. He comes alive under my pencil.

Truly my beloved Regional children have become as my own flesh and blood. As Kipling's Mowgli said, "We be of one blood, thou and I" and this enabled him to communicate with all the creatures of the jungle. So have I become blood-kin with my Regional children, with Joanda and Suzette, with Dick Wagner and Billy Honeycutt, with Birdie Boyer, homeless Judy and all the rest. There is only one way to write my books—to live the child's life with him. The child's living presence, his spirit, must be my guide, first, last and always.

Being one with them, not an alien adult from another world, but a sympathetic soul sharing their eager curiosity, their faith and ready acceptance of an uncertain world, their hopes and joys as well as their problems and sorrows—because children in even the most undesirable environments and deplorable conditions are never entirely bereft of hope—all this sharing becomes a part of the creative process.

And so a living drama must have its roots in living.

It becomes a mirror held up to life. And because it takes from life, so should it reflect back to life. It should be rich in all its implications for the discerning child reader. Such a child, living in a totally unlike environment, reading such a book, should be able to reach out beyond his narrow horizon and live the life of the book's hero, even as the author lived it. He is able to forget his own smug comfort and satisfaction and selfishness, project himself into a new sort of life never experienced before, a life with some sorrow or tragedy perhaps, but through it all, to share in the hero's courage, fortitude and endurance, and thus in the reading, take new courage unto himself. Through such a book he experiences the feel and the flavor of a life very different from his own, and in the sharing, widens his own powers of love, compassion and understanding.

The creating of books is a varied process. There are as many ways of creating books as there are authors. I speak for myself alone. Creating books which reflect the many varied ways of life in our country, with all the honesty and courage and sympathy at my command, has been a pleasure and a great privilege.

A Story from Strangers

CHAIN AROUND MY HEART

Strange lands are chained around my heart;
Strange ways unknown before,
Now forever mine,
Around my heart
like tendrils twine.

What difference is it how we speak,
or eat or dress or talk,
if love can bind us close
and guide us as we walk?

HOW WONDERFUL to come back to a college campus and feel young again, and to that heart of the college, its library. It seems strange to me that my papers and manuscripts and illustrations should have found a permanent home in a university library, when I think that they were written for three and four-year-olds and ten and twelve-year-olds. I cannot get used to the idea, but I am deeply grateful.

I always get a shock when a college student or graduate or parent tells me, "I had your books when I was small." It is hard for me to realize that a second and soon a third generation of children will be reading my books. They don't seem to wear out or go stale!

It seems such a short time since I was a student in college myself, specializing not in English as my high school English teacher had advised me to do, saying, "I feel sure you will do some form of creative work," but taking all the art courses I could get. Such a short time since I was in art school in New York, working half-days trying to learn how to draw, and visiting publishers trying to get jobs—any kind of job, anything to illustrate, to earn enough to pay my tuition and expenses to go on studying. Such a short time since my little son played automobile every day with his little friends, and gave me the idea for Mr. Small and so many other ideas to put into picture books. Such a short time since I first came south out of a raging blizzard, arriving in Lakeland to find summer sunshine and blooming flowers, heaven in the middle of winter! Since I first came south and saw America for the first time and got the idea for my Regional books, to let children know how other children live, work and play all over our country. I can hardly believe that I have actually done fifteen Regionals and ten Roundabouts, but what a wonderful experience it has been—one that I want to share with you.

Each of us has his own America, the America we have seen, known or read about. Sometimes it is as small as our own back yard and it may even have a high board fence around it, so high we cannot see over. Sometimes it is as wide as the country itself, stretching "from sea to shining sea!" Sometimes, alas, we travel from coast to coast, hit only a few high spots, returning no wiser than before.

Back in the 1940's when I first began exploring America, two questions were often asked me. First, "Are you selling something?" because I carried a little gray zipper bag with me. Second, "Are you on vacation?" Why, otherwise, should a gray-haired woman be sitting on a street corner or beside a country road on a camp stool, making drawings in a sketch book? It was a little hard to explain!

But after I overcame my first timidity and got used to being an object of curiosity, how wonderful it was to go among strangers and find they were not strange, but warm and human and lovable; to go among strangers, hostile and disapproving perhaps at first, and to break down the barrier of hardness and bitterness and prejudice by an example of love. "Come in and rest a while!" may seem a strange greeting from a total stranger. I heard it often, from people I had been told were hateful and suspicious of outsiders. "Come in and eat. We haven't much, but what we have you're plumb welcome to." "Night's a-comin' on. Please stay here with us. It's too late to get back to town." How can you help but love people who say these things to you?

In your own environment, you are one like all the others. In a strange environment, you are the stranger. The others are all alike; you are unlike and different. This is an experience we should all have for our own growth and development.

Wherever I went I found that people liked to tell me about themselves. I seemed to invite confidence. Seated in a bus beside a stranger, I learned his whole life history. Children loved to have interviews with me and tell me their adventures. The highest compliment I was ever paid was in the cotton country, when they said of me, "Miss Lenski is as common as she can be!"

The word "common" is an arresting one, in its old Elizabethan meaning. It does not mean "ordinary" or "inferior" or "beneath one," but "earthy," "wholesome" or "good." When you share people's joys and sorrows, sympathize with them in their trials and difficulties, love and admire them for their courage and fortitude in the face of adversity, it is a rich experience indeed.

I am often asked: How do I do it? Other authors have told me they would have no idea how to start getting a story in a strange place where they had never been before. How do I get a story from strangers? There are two ways. First, by invitation, and second, without. The first is much easier, of course. The second, without invitation, is much more difficult.

You go as a stranger, just as you are. In my case, with camp-stool, sketch book and pencil. *Bayou Suzette* and *Strawberry Girl,* my first two Regionals, were done in this way, for I knew no other. I went as an artist, making drawings. Children, then adults became curious and asked me questions. I asked them questions in return and jotted down their answers. Children were my best informants; through them, I was invited into the homes. The rest was easy.

Did I tell them I was writing a book? Yes and No. Sometimes I did, sometimes I did not. It depended on the person and the situation. A few people might resent being written about, but they are in the minority. I let them alone, for there are so many more who are eager and anxious to "be in a book." When I work in the schools, there is keen competition to be hero or heroine. My choice is a difficult one, for I do not like to show favoritism.

In 1947, after *Strawberry Girl* had won the Newbery Medal, I received my first invitation. Letters from a rural school in Arkansas said: "We are the cotton children. We pick cotton. Nobody has ever written about us. Won't you come and do it?" All that winter they wrote me letters about their cotton experiences. At Christmas time, the teacher sent me recordings of the children's voices. I went and was received with open arms. All the doors were opened to me. I made two visits, one in the spring and one in the fall when cotton was being harvested.

In the school, the children volunteered to "tell me things," from the fifth and sixth grades down to the second. Everybody was excited, all wanted to help. Each day I was bombarded with questions: "Got that cotton book wrote yet?" "Got that cotton book done?" They did not realize how long it takes to write a book. They had to wait two years before they held copies in their hands, copies they had picked cotton to buy—the first books they had ever owned. How they loved it—every detail true to their own experiences. "I told her that! I told her that!" they cried.

While I was there I put on a sunbonnet, went out in the fields with them, achieved a sunburned nose and an aching back and about half as much cotton as the average ten-year-old could pick. But I was doing more than picking cotton. I was listening and looking harder than ever in my life. I was trying to fix every detail of action and speech and mood in my mind permanently, never to be forgotten.

I interviewed twenty-five or more families, sharecropper, tenant and owner alike. I had meals with them, learned to know the parents, rode the trucks with the men back and forth to the gin and participated in every detail of their life. They accepted me as one of themselves. When it was time to go, I could hardly tear myself away. I had to board the train for St. Louis at a town four miles south of the school, during school hours, when the children could not see me off. Some kind friend arranged with the engineer of the train to go slowly past the crossing near the school.

I went out on the rear platform, with a large, white, man's handkerchief. There they were, all my cotton children, standing in the road, waving goodbye. I waved as long as I could see them, then returned to my seat in the train and had a good cry. The children cried too, even the boys—they wrote me afterwards.

Their lives had never been made important before.

Out on the wind-swept, snowbound prairie in South Dakota, in the winter of 1949 and '50, a group of children huddled over the register of a pipeless furnace on the floor of the schoolroom, trying to keep warm, while their teacher, Ruth Carter, read them the book *Strawberry Girl.* They were studying Florida in their social studies. I was in Florida when their letter reached me, a letter of invitation. With it came a photograph of rosy-cheeked children in heavy winter clothes sitting on the steps of the schoolhouse. What beautiful, healthy-looking children, I thought. How I would love to write about them! That winter and the next I received letters from teacher and pupils that were a real American epic—their rugged experiences coping with the weather in getting back and forth to school. Theirs was an invitation I had to accept. At the end of May I went to South Dakota, heard their tales first hand, tried to get the feel of the prairie and sense the lives of the children who knew it so much better than I, so that I might write about them. My book, *Prairie School* pays tribute, I hope, to these valiant children and to their dedicated teacher, who literally gave up her life for them. Younger teachers would not accept a position in such a school, so she kept on . . . and died, a few years later, of cancer.

A year or so later, Iowa children in a rural school near Remsen, reading *Prairie School,* invited me to visit their corn-farms, and *Corn-Farm Boy* was the result. So one book has led to another, an endless chain. It has been gratifying to me, to feel that American children themselves have been carrying on the Regional series.

But some of the books have been done without benefit of invitation. For fifteen years I had been wanting to do a story of the Amish people of Pennsylvania, who are and have been for two hundred years, a part of the fabric of American life, but I did not know where to go. I had no contact, no lead. I waited and waited . . . hopefully, but nothing came. Then I was invited to speak at a summer reading conference at the University of Pennsylvania. This is it, this is my call to the Amish, I thought. I went, the teachers offered to help me find a location, but nothing came of it. So my hopes were dashed. I was to get no lead, it seemed. I would have to do it the hard way—from scratch.

An artist friend who lived west of Philadelphia, on the edge of the Amish country, invited me for a visit and took me for a drive. We came to a little red schoolhouse where Amish children were playing in the yard. It was my setting come to life. I went in and introduced myself to the non-Amish teacher. She had not heard my name and did not know my books, but she was friendly and sympathetic. She sent me to an Amish woman, who approved of what I wanted to do and helped me in every way possible. She took me with her to House-Amish church, she found a perfect Amish family with nine children who invited me into their home. She answered hundreds of my questions and made my book possible. She even suggested the title *Shoo-Fly Girl.* After the book was published, she gave it her entire approval.

I wish I could tell you about some of the real people whom I have known and loved, who have become characters in my books. For *Strawberry Girl,* there was Birdie Boyer in a field near Lakeland, plowing with an old white mule. There was Shoestring who "never couldn't git no fat on his bones," wearing overalls and black felt hat. I met him at a stock auction outside of town where he was ushering the animals in and out of the ring. He took me to his home to see his pet coon and instructed me in Cracker methods of fishing and catching alligators. In *Blue Ridge Billy,* the real Billy rode his mule up to my back kitchen door—we had rented a house in the mountains for the month of December. His little sisters came to our frozen spring to get water, dressed in cotton dresses, their bare legs blue with cold. And Joanda in the cotton fields, the most real of all my book people, not in school but out in the field picking all day. She had a beautiful but sad face which told the whole cotton story.

My adult characters are real too. Old Man Dunnaway sang "Jaybird Sittin' on a Swingin' Limb" aloud to me at the farmers' market in Lakeland. Grandpa Robinson in *Boom Town Boy,* who had made millions in oil, still lived in his chicken coop, where I talked to him. Charlie Boy in *Texas Tomboy,* a woman grown, who told me all her questionable childhood adventures and shared with me her fierce loyalty to her beloved ranch. Mama Hattie whose ups-and-downs I shared for over two years in her home and my own. All these people were real. I could never have invented them or the things that happened to them.

A few more details: In each region where I go, I take copious notes, and I fill a sketch book with sketches. I have to be all eyes, all ears, all heart and soul. I have to be able to take in my surroundings at a glance, to remember all I see and hear, for it is often impossible to get it down on paper. I have to listen to people talking to me, remember how they say their words, for there is colorful speech being used in all parts of our country. I have to size up the people, study their character and sense their personality. It is an engrossing, absorbing and wearing process which often depletes one physically and spiritually.

This effort to project oneself into another's life, this effort to see things from his point of view, to understand why he does what he does when he does, to feel at one with him, is not easy. Sharing some of his experiences can be soul-shaking;

sharing some children's experiences is heart-breaking and keeps one sleepless at night. The emotional pull is tremendous. Because it is so strong, one can only hope that it will carry over into the book itself, that the reader can feel it and enter into the lives of the characters as the author has done.

What is the purpose of getting books from life? Why not get them from the imagination? Why not use imaginary characters and imaginary situations? Why not get them from inside, "expressing yourself", instead of from the outside?

I believe that in these troubled times of unrest, what the world needs most is understanding, what people need is understanding, what children need is understanding of others. We have hundreds of imaginative books for children, but all too few that present human relations problems with real people for characters, and which show how problems in human relations can be resolved. Children need many kinds of books, but what they need most of all are books that help them to learn how to live.

Children should be consciously taught how to get along with their own parents, with their brothers and sisters, with friends and relatives, with strangers, and with people they have never seen; with people who are like themselves and with people who are different. One of the best ways to teach them is through books. The wear and tear of human relations comes to us all and we must somehow work our way through it and acquire a peaceful and Christian approach to living.

Getting books from life is a rich experience for the author, and because my books are honest interpretations of many ways of life, I hope they will enrich the lives of the children who read them. By reading of the way a hero or heroine meets a problem or situation in a book, and by identifying himself with the hero, the reader should be able to find the help he needs in his own life.

I try to arouse in my readers a feeling of loving compassion for people in all walks of life, which will stay with them and influence them as long as they live. A book, I believe, should do more than entertain or amuse. It should illumine the whole adventure of living.

Place and People

LAND SO STRANGE

When first I saw that land so strange,
Never alien was I there.
Despite the newness, love I felt,
Knitting me close
to make me aware,

To see with the eyes of the people there,
To sense the sorrows that they bear,
To share their joys and happiness,
To speak with loving care.

FIRST THE CHATTER of many voices, then the coming and going of many people. They settle down, the lights dim, a hush descends. The Listener sits back in his seat, expectantly waiting. The curtain rises, the lights brighten, the drama begins. A story of American life is told.

Supper is ready. The children come running in and take their places. Father sits down, and Mother places food on the table. A short prayer is spoken. Warmth and happiness fill the room, perhaps even tears or laughter.

Dusk falls and the lamp is lighted. A kerosene lamp or a high-powered electric bulb. What does it matter? Outside the windows perhaps deep woods can be seen, or rolling hills, or apartment houses on a crowded street. Outside—the quiet hush of a sleepy countryside, the barking of a neighbor's dog, the roar of wind over a mountain pass, or the mechanical clatter of a noisy city. What does it matter? Within, the room sings with the drama of family life.

The Listener, in seat below, quiet, alert, drinking it all in.

The scene varies—perhaps a father is absent, or a child is lost, a mother sick or unworthy of her trust. Perhaps children are thoughtless and unappreciative, parents lacking in understanding. The home is well-furnished or ill, the children have much or little of material things, of food to eat, of clothes to wear, depending on the economic status of the parents and their ability to challenge their environment. Perhaps the children are over-indulged and pampered; they may have just enough; or the parents may be away at work all day; or they may lead lives of luxury and leisure.

But the home—underneath all the outward differences—the home is the heart of security for the children. It may not even have a roof—it may be a tent, a trailer, a boat, a quonset hut, a tumble-down shack. American children live in them all. They sleep, some on the ground, some on the hard floor, others on resilient springs under softest eiderdown.

The Listener senses the setting and feels at home there. He sits back and drinks in the words, savoring each and hoarding them like treasure. Through words, the story, the plot, the drama takes form.

Perhaps it is a gay and happy story, perhaps it is sad and thoughtful, or it may be poignant and heart-rending. The Listener is transported into the lives of others. He lives with them in their particular setting—on lofty mountain, in crowded city, on farm, ranch or river, in cotton field or peach orchard. He shares their struggles and their joys, his concern over their fate is actively aroused until the final curtain goes down. He has forgotten himself and his selfish concerns for a while. He has been enriched by the experience of entering the lives of others.

The play is enacted for the benefit of the Listener. The Listener in turn will pass it on to others through the medium of the printed word. From the initial staging and rehearsal, through the pulsing, vibrating performance, the play is transmitted vicariously to the Listener, or author, whose concern is then to relay it to others that they too may share in vicarious living.

Just how this is done, we shall try to explain. The Listener says in effect—where I have been, what I have seen and heard and felt on the stage of life, there you, the reader, may go also. He says: I was there. This is how it was. Come with me. You may share it too.

The Listener's task is to convey: first, the Sense of Place; and second, the Sense of Life. As Sean O'Casey, the Irish playwright has so wisely said: "The artist's place is to be wherever life is, active life, found in neither ivory tower nor concrete shelter; he must be out listening to everything, looking at everything, and thinking it all out afterwards."

Kay Boyle, the novelist, has said: "Who can live in a country without knowing what the people living in it think? The part of the writer is to fuse himself with man, to speak for all men, or else to speak to all men of a common experience."

And so the Listener-author goes to a chosen setting to get his story.

The love of one's own home and surroundings

is a natural instinct and a powerful one. Homesickness is a strange word with many meanings. Away from home, from the familiar setting of one's life, a person can be engulfed by physical and spiritual sickness. Cutting one's ties with the familiar can be a terrifying experience, the pull of the familiar is so strong. A person identifies, he is part of the place where he was born and where his roots were first put down.

But the same loyalty and devotion can be built up for other places, too, as one's experience widens. The traveler learns the meaning of the word adjustment, he learns to be at home anywhere. The little world of his birthplace gives way to the wider world of experience. And as he moves about, he cultivates a love of many places, places he loves to visit, where he can enjoy peace and contentment, building up an attachment equal to that he once felt only for his original native home. He identifies with many places, each of which may be different from the other.

But there is a third kind of identification or *Kinship with Place.*

The Listener, the author, confronted by a strange setting, alien to him in appearance and meaning, expecting perhaps to be repelled or at least to suffer an uncomfortable period of adjustment, feels instead a warm welcome. At first sight, the place is magic—he falls in love with it. It has a strange instantaneous, unaccountable appeal. From the very first moment when he gets off a plane or steps out of a car, he senses the newness but a welcome in the very newness of this so-different world. He hears it say: Come! I am waiting for you! Why were you so long in coming?

He stops for a moment, abashed, astonished. Then he comes forward, whispering: Ah yes! This is what I want. This is my place. I belong here. The curtain is going up, the drama is about to begin. My story is waiting for me.

It may not be the appeal of physical setting, which may even be repellent; nor of the people he meets—their faces are hard, they are yet strangers. He looks around bewildered, everything is strange and different—he has never been here before. But his own home is far away and completely forgotten now, here . . . a warm welcome claims him.

He stares at the differences—in setting, in custom and habit of the people. He knows he can never take these to himself. The place, the people, the houses, the landscape—they are all so different.

The stranger's floor is full of knots,
His rooms are empty, bare;
The stranger's clothes are not like mine,
I look at him and stare.

Then he remembers:

But the stranger has a heart like mine,
His face betrays no guile;
He has his loves, his hates, his fears—
I look at him and smile.

The Place cries out to him—its very difference seems unique. He is filled with a violent awareness of all that it offers. He is filled with a strange content, a kinship with strangers never felt before.

Drawn by a magnet,
Struck by a dart,
Held by a chain
I could not pull apart.
Breath of my breath,
Life of my life to be,
Closer than my bloodstream
Is this land to me.

Kinship with strangeness—
I've been here before,

This is my home
And will be evermore.
Closer than a mother,
This land of mine to be,
When I gave it my heart,
It gave itself to me.

And so a Sense of Place develops, felt strongly in many regions. A great love for:

the sweep and roll of the brown prairie land,
the bare rocky boldness of the parched desert,
the intimacy of lush green hills and valleys along the course of a winding river,
the straight rows of trees in orange grove or apple orchard,
the miracle of growth in cornland or grassland.

The Listener hears the rush of wind in the desert, the raucous call of the crow over the cornfield, the sweet song of the mocking-bird through a moonlight night. He scans the sky studying the weather. He lives each day as if he too had been born in this place and had never known anything different. And so he develops a special awareness; he sees how tightly the place is bound up with the people, and has shaped them to its liking. He learns that a landscape in its many moods can take on the character of drama, and portend tragedy, happiness, humor or grief of the people, taking on almost human properties.

What place is this I love so well?
Its very spirit I can tell,
though it is new to me.
I seem to love it more and more,
Though here I have not been before.

What place is this, so strange, so new?
The trees are wrong, the fences too.
Who has set the roads askew?
Houses odd and faces new,
So unlike all those I knew.

But yet I seem to know it well,
Somehow it sets for me a spell
of tantalizing tenderness,
of softness under dire distress,
Until I feel it all my own,
A place I've somehow surely known.

The place so strange draws me along,
It gives me love, so I belong,
The faces new a secret show
Which they, unsaid, want me to know,

The author tries to transmit this Sense of Place—of geography, if you will—to the reader in words.

In *Bayou Suzette* I want my readers to feel

with me the mystery of the great cypress swamps, hung with dismal mysterious curtains of Spanish moss; to feel the dampness, the wetness of the bayous in this land that is more water than land; to feel it so vividly that the very moisture seems to ooze out of their skins.

In *Strawberry Girl,* the Sense of Place means sand and sunshine.

Git sand in your shoes,
You can never git it out;
That's one thing I know
With nary a doubt.

Git sun in your heart,
From sunshine never part.
Land of sand and sunshine,
of sparkling water,
waving palm,
Land of singing bird,
Of blooming plant and tree,
Who, of those who love it,
Would want to part from thee?

Git sand in your shoes,
You can never git it out;
That's one thing I know
With nary a doubt.

I have written several stories about life in the piney woods of Southeastern states.

Out in the piney woods
By a branch that winds
in and out among tall trees,
Where the sweet scent
of pine needles
floats on the breeze;

A roof over our heads,
water from the spring,
fuel from the piney woods
to burn in the stove.
Home in the piney woods—
that's what I love.

Home, home in the piney woods,
Where the scent of pine needles
blows sweet on the breeze,
Home in the piney woods—
That's where I live.

In *Texas Tomboy,* I want my readers to suffer the dryness of the drouth as Charlie Boy did. "The taste of dust was dry in her mouth," or as the cowboys said, "We can almost spit cotton!" I want my reader

to dream of the rain that never seemed to come,
to feel dryness on the tongue even when taking a drink,
to try to keep clean when there is no water to wash in,

to realize that wasting a single drop of water is
a crime.

I want all my readers to rejoice, when at last the rains come and the terrible drouth comes to an end.

In *Prairie School,* I want my readers to feel
the awful hazards of the blizzard,
the risks of being buried in snowbanks,
the coldness of the cold, cold snow,
the lashing of the gale when the lariat rope had to be tied to the school house door to get it shut,
the boiling of snow to get water to drink,
and the many uses of the snow-water, too precious to be squandered.

Swift are the prairie children,
Riding across the plain;
From rise of sun
Till day is done,
Careless of snow or rain.

Strong are the prairie children,
Pushing against the breeze;
Their feet have trod
The prairie sod,
They know not fear nor ease.

Brave are the prairie children,
Wading the whirling snow;
Born of the wind,
Born of the sun,
Over the prairie they go!

This is a Sense of Place, a sense of human Geography, the strong bond that ties people to their environment and makes them what they are in character and personality.

Kinship with Place leads us on to a Sense of Life or Kinship with People.

One cannot have a story, or create a drama, without the principal actors, people. Even as a place can be strange at first acquaintance, so can people.

People of different habits and customs and beliefs, people of different racial strains and color of skin, can be difficult to understand. But even as a place beckons the writer on, offering him a welcome, so do the strange people whom he has never seen before. They may invite him on even through their indifference, abuse, rudeness or repulsion. Such qualities may only serve as bait to lure him on, all the more determined to fathom their secrets and to try to find out how and why they became what they are—what shaped them for good or evil, what forces they had to meet and how they did it.

There is a story in their lives. Each day in the life of any family in any situation offers drama. Will the writer have the wit, the sensitivity, the persistence, the understanding and imagination necessary to draw it out? He never knows. All he can do is to proceed, to make haste slowly, to hope . . . and to pray. Unless he can enter their lives, there will be no story.

A story is set down in black letters on a printed page. How did it get there? Whence did it come? How does a drama get written? My own way is to go to life itself, to go to the people I want to write about and get the story from them. I am only an intermediary. It is they who put life on the printed page.

The great novels for adults have always glorified the art of living, they have portrayed the living spirit of man. They have given truthful pictures of man's daily life over the ages. Along with the vivid exactness of documentation has been combined the art of infusing facts with spirit. The novelist interprets human beings not only through their outward behavior, but through the workings of their mind and heart.

To enter the mind and heart of another is a rare art, indeed. The Sense of Life must be put down on paper. How is this done?

It is not done by introspection or by personal withdrawal from life. Nor is it done by trusting to one's powers of imagination. It can only be done by complete self-abnegation and self-forgetfulness; this alone enables one to enter the life of another. Only through empathy can one learn to understand others. Exactness, truthful portrayal of place, the concrete presentation of facts, becomes glorified, illuminated by the spirit. A chair takes on the shape of the sitter, an old coat takes on the personality of the wearer, vocabulary reflects character, inanimate objects reflect human qualities. Empathy is imagination of the highest order, because it projects itself into the life of another.

I am grateful to William James for the word *otherness*. Otherness becomes a boomerang. One must first lose oneself to find oneself.

How does an Author write about living people?

The Author is not yet an Author. He is still

the Listener. He goes to the people and listens. He writes down what he hears. He asks questions about things they know better than he. He offers friendship, uncritical sympathy. There is something about being a Listener that invites confidence. And so he fills notebook and sketchbook, one after the other, jotting down words and sentences, sketching place and people, landscapes, houses, objects, all the visual background as well as action; jotting down pages and pages of conversation as it falls on his unaccustomed ears.

This is not as easy as it sounds. Some people are unresponsive; some are suspicious or uncooperative; there are barriers to be broken down and this can only be done by an honest, straightforward approach, tempered by sympathy and humility. It is a devastating and exhausting experience, physically and emotionally, to try to enter another's life . . . How is it done? How can I explain? First, I must say it is frankly impossible.

Can one ever get close to a stranger? To an enemy? Can any one really enter another's life? No—or probably not. Even though we make every effort, do we not only project our own self into the other self? Yes, I'm afraid so. And yet, the main pre-requisite is complete self-extinction, a step beyond self-forgetfulness. One must wipe oneself out. Can this be done? I do not know. I have tried. . . not consciously, but involuntarily I have sometimes reached a stage of near self-extinction and had to be re-called back to myself. But I still say it cannot be done.

All the Listener can do is try. The Listener is facing the People. What are they thinking? What kind of lives are they leading? They start talking. The same kind of spontaneous awareness that greets the newcomer at his first sight of the unknown Place, now engulfs him. . .

My nerves tingle, my heart pounds, my pencil shakes, I can hardly take notes and many, afterwards, will be illegible and useless. My mind does not control what my hand is doing, my hand is responding automatically. I am fearful of missing a shade of meaning, a colorful word not in my own vocabulary, an expressive gesture or facial expression, a gleam of hope flashing out of a look of despair . . . it all happens so fast, my memory is staggered . . . I must get it down or I will forget. A fearful sense of urgency presses me on. Everything happens at once, as drama is performed before me, words flying, arguments, actions, people coming and going . . . through the confusion I must never lose sight of the heart of the drama.

I am shaken . . . I can get down only a few high-spots, a few key-words. Ah yes, here is the secret: KEY WORDS, symbols of all that is taking place. If I can get them down, I will have it.

Key words—keys to open the door to another life,
keys to the action and drama, to the visual scene,
to the tension of emotion.
Key words, yes it is these that interpret a region,
that exalt even a humble way of life
Keys to the interpretation of a human being
and the life he lives in the setting that shaped him.

Helen Keller's first word was WATER. That word was the KEY that opened up the world of thought and expression to the blind, deaf and dumb girl and revolutionized her life.

Sylvia Ashton Warner, a dedicated teacher in New Zealand, tells of her experiences with Maori children in her book *Spinster.* Because words like *come* and *look* conveyed no emotion, she built up a key vocabulary to teach her children to read. Her key words were: *Mommy, Daddy, kiss, cry, ghost,* and others not so respectable or pleasant, like *police, frightened, bomb, jail, fight.* These words had meaning in their lives and speeded up the learning-to-read process.

UNESCO teachers, working with people in famine areas, teaching them to read, started with words of intense meaning: *crop, soil, hunger, manure.*

Key words have intense meaning. They are a part of dynamic life, a part of the very *stuff* of life. Note the word *stuff,* a very old key word. When I was in the cotton region and the children were contributing ideas for my cotton book, I was amused and startled when a little girl said, "I got to tell Miss Lenski a lot of *stuff,* so she can write that book." She did not know how truly she spoke. Key words portray the very *stuff* of life.

Sometimes the Listener's records must be kept hidden, for fear of causing self-consciousness, which will stop the flow of revelation, and may hinder the sharing of a life. So the Listener learns to take down notes surreptitiously without looking at the pad, with the pad hidden behind a convenient purse . . . until I am caught in my tricks by a candid child who pipes up:

"How can you write without looking at the paper?"

Child, child, long ago I learned to write in the dark. My hand needs no eye, it sees of itself. It needs no ME to tell it what to do. The ME does not exist any more. My hand is automatic. My hand becomes a physical bond between two living spirits . . .

Sometimes the Listener feels ashamed to be a witness to the baring of a soul, unasked-for, freely offered. The hand falters, hesitates, stops writing, but the words and sentences, key words and sentences, etched not in pencil but in acid, etched in the memory never to be forgotten, to stay there always and to come back again and again with all the force and power of a shout heard around the world, to haunt the author as long as she walks the earth.

Words, key sentences, never to be forgotten, nor the tone of voice, nor the facial expression, words that keep my child heroes and heroines ever young in heart even though in real life they have reached adulthood and themselves long ago forgotten a youthful confession . . . Key sentences that tell the story of a life:

A five-year-old girl in Louisiana:

"My Maman's got a leetle girl dead!" followed by a dramatic tale of a little sister falling in the bayou and drowning.

A ten-year-old migrant girl with heartbreak in her voice: "She told me I couldn't come to her party in my feedsack dress. She told me I wasn't invited!"

An eight-year-old cotton picker: "The bossman's wife said, 'I told Dave to keep the kids out of the barn! Now he's run over him!' "

A twelve-year-old prairie boy: "The cattle were gone—lost in the blizzard. I had to go find 'em."

A girl in the Texas drouth: "Will it ever rain again, Pa? Will it . . . ever . . . rain again?"

And the quiet voice of a piney-woods child: "I couldn't go to school. I didn't have no shoes to wear."

Simple sentences, key sentences like a cry of pain, that hold all the tragedy and grief, courage and stoicism of childhood.

Key sentences that pummel and pound on one's consciousness, that make one's heart beat fast and give one no rest, that leave one limp and exhausted . . . so that one must run from this hard-fought reality, indulge oneself in insensibility for a time, become comatose, rejecting, erasing all outside stimuli . . . Rest, rest, peace and quiet, a respite before taking stock again, recovering one's equanimity and going forth afresh and restored on this wild adventure of understanding others, of sharing others' lives, not only the good, but the bad, the fright and the fear, the joy and the triumph of the great adventure of living.

But there are interruptions, all around me the sound of many voices, extraneous voices, trying to explain things to me, to tell me what I ought to know. I am tactfully impatient. I must wait till they subside. These words, well-meant, deflect me from my purpose. They go on and on, but I hear them not. I recede into my shell, as if I am hiding in the shadow, as if I were invisible.

Ah yes, in the early days I often wished for a disguise to wear when I go among strangers, an invisible coat to hide my real self, to be more truly one of them, to see and not to be seen, to hear and not be heard, to feel and sense and live with them as they do themselves, as they would if I were nowhere around. But in lieu of such disguise, which I have never yet achieved, I fade away, I lose my identity, reach a state where I—the real ME—no longer exists; where I forget who I am and where I came from, what my usual life is and what my purpose is in coming . . . I am no longer a person, I am an intermediary, a sounding board, a mere link in a chain, I take on the personality of the place, of the person. I sink my soul in his.

I must be alone with the place and the people . . . with the aloneness of the prairie . . . all the long evening, all the long night, all the long ensuing day, with only the soaring song of the meadow lark for company . . . and thus *I become the prairie . . .*

I try to sense the Otherness
Of people strange to me;
Very different do they look,
How queer they seem to be.

And then the newness fades,
When as myself I see them clear;
I share their thoughts, their very life,
And they are friends so dear.

Gone is the sense of Otherness,
When as myself I can them see;
In sharing sorrows, joys and hopes,
They are the same as me.

Ah, there it is. That is how it is done.

But, you protest, that is only the beginning. You have only gotten the material. What about writing the story?

There is a simple answer. The story now writes itself. Absorbed and saturated in the Place and the People, the writing of the story, always done away from the actual setting, is easy. The Listener turned Author has communed so deeply with Place and People, this communion will surely seep into the unconscious and come out in the final expression. At least that is his hope. He uses no magic but that of kindness, no miracles but those of forgiveness and compassion.

This is the way it was in this Place. This is the Truth. These things happened to the people. Where I have gone and what I have sensed, I will give to my readers.

Land that never knew my birthplace,
Land accepted, chosen, prized;
Land unlike my native region,
By adoption realized.

Land unknown but never alien,
Land so new of me a part;
Once I gave it understanding,
There I buried roots and heart.

Gift by Proxy

STRANGENESS

Strangeness is a funny thing,
It makes you feel so queer,
Till it becomes familiar,
And then you hold it dear.

Strangeness makes one cautious,
Afraid of each small move,
Until we make it welcome
By meeting it with love.

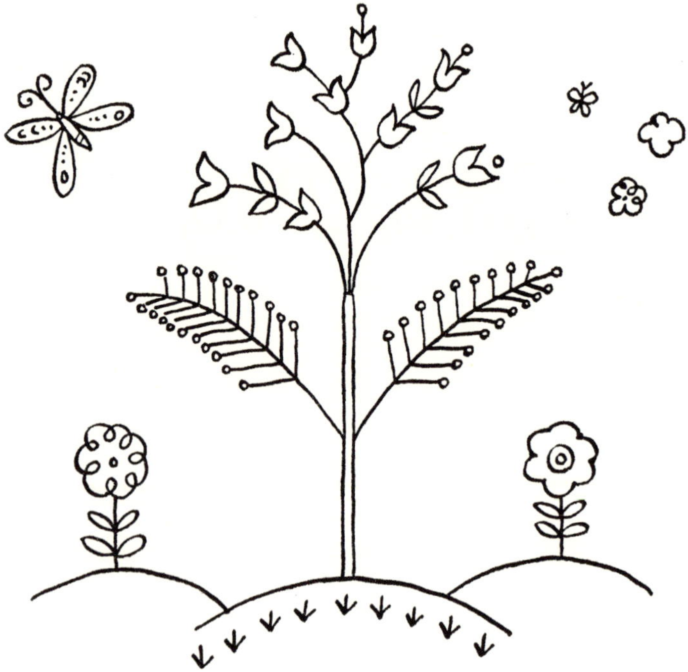

WHAT IS A BOOK? Some pages of paper placed between two covers, pages with printed words on them, words of little or great potential. What is a book for? A book is to read. It is something from which we get information, amusement or entertainment. It is something to give delight and humor, and oh so much more—to enrich life itself.

How are books created? How are they written? How do they come into being? A story is a story and always has been since the beginning of time. Long before printing was ever invented, stories were handed down by word of mouth from one generation to the next. A story is still a story. A grandmother tells a story to her grandchildren, tells them what she did as a little girl and they think it is wonderful. Daddy makes up a story about a bear for the children at bedtime and adds a new chapter every night. It tests all of Daddy's invention, and the children think it is wonderful. A beginning author works a whole week and writes ten pages and feels sure it ought to be published. The embryo author struggles and struggles to create a story, out of a void probably, or takes a course in creative writing to find out how it is done. Books are written in many ways, as many ways as there are authors, but in the main, they come from two sources, from within and from without.

Writing from WITHIN is most common. In the teaching of creative writing, the emphasis is on self-expression. What is inside you must be brought out. There is only one trouble with this method. If there is little or nothing inside you, how can you express it?

Writing from WITHOUT, from the outside, means a study of living people and their lives apart from oneself. Instead of a selfish, egocentric occupation, writing becomes an act of true dedication and service to others. A book can be the product of a lifetime of loving compassion for other people.

Writing from the INSIDE is a good way to evade writing from the OUTSIDE. It often becomes a retreat from life itself. The author "stews in his own juices." Wordsworth said:

> *"The world is too much with us; late and soon,*
> *Getting and spending we lay waste our powers;*
> *Little we see in Nature that is ours."*

In the whole field of the creative arts, there is an unfortunate but popular trend away from OUTSIDE expression into INSIDE introspection. This leads to definite evasions in all forms of art. The artist or painter who can see no beauty in the commonplace has to resort to splashing meaningless blobs on his canvas. The novelist and playwright who is out of step with everyday life has to resort to the depiction of degeneracy and vice. The poet who is out of touch with the beauty of living, tries to fool us with a hodgepodge of meaningless words, with incoherencies which desecrate the name of poetry. Introspection is always unhealthy and destructive.

The children's author who finds the child's

life dull and not worth writing about resorts to evasions and contortions of the art of Pollyanna living, or indulges his own feeble imaginings in the name of fantasy, or retreats into the romantic past. Of course, if you do not know anything about people and their lives and have no desire to find out, then all you can do is to resort to evasions and call it art.

The author has to make a choice of what he wants to write about. Is he going to create from the INSIDE or from the OUTSIDE? One is easy, the other difficult. Which path will he take? Authors are timid souls, really. The chief reason why most of them choose the INSIDE is a lack of courage to face the OUTSIDE. They cannot face the present. They are scared of the life of today. They see only its tragedy, its violence, its ruthlessness as a thing to be exploited or to be ignored. Sean O'Casey says: "They are afraid of life's full-throated shouting." Present-day life is not cute, not pretty, not romantic.

Authors are lazy too, I'm sorry to say. It is far easier to sit at your desk and concoct an implausible story in your head than to go out and face strangers in a strange environment and get a story. It is far easier to write an imaginative story than to try to project yourself into the life of another. I know. I've done both. I can write an imaginative story in a week. To write a Regional will take me a year. Yes, authors are afraid of life, so they have found means of escape. Rather than face life, they retreat, first, into the past; their own or the historical past. Second, into the imagination; third, into artificial life.

Retreat into the past can take two forms: first, a nostalgic memory of one's own past; or, second, the historical past.

Some of our children's authors claim that they get their knowledge and understanding of children out of memories of their own childhood instead of from real children. Most authors begin this way. I did myself. I wrote my first two books out of my own childhood. Many fine books have been written in this way and I hold them in due honor and respect. But some authors go no farther and this is a pity. For nostalgic memories of childhood, seen through the glamorized glow of adult memory, are often unreliable and unduly glorified. Memory is kind, memory is charitable, memory is merciful. It conveniently lets slip the unpleasant and magnifies the pleasant. It sifts the good from the bad and rejects the bad.

Recently I have been reviewing my own childhood and I have been astonished. I had a good childhood, I know that. But was it all "sweetness and light?" I confess if there was unpleasantness, it has all faded away. My memory has been accomodating and handed down to me only joy and beauty.

So I wonder, I cannot help wondering how well-rounded a book is when it grows out of the memory of one's own past. Needless to say, such books are beautiful, especially to nostalgic adults, and they find a permanent place in our affections. But they should not be the only ones written for children.

Retreat into the historical past means writing stories of *"the olden days."* Ah! it's fun to write about the olden days, about little girls in hoop skirts and pretty bonnets, about spinning wheels and candle sticks! There is a tendency to see life through rose-tinted glasses. The past achieves a patina of glamor which camouflages actual facts. Here, the author retreats into the library and does research. He studies his chosen period and reads all the books he can find about it. He gets his story from other books and not from real life. Nostalgic memory and repetition play active parts.

True, there are many accurate records of life lived in the past, many first hand accounts to be found in primary sources. But secondary sources are repetitious. Each person copies what somebody else has previously said, and some gross inaccuracies have thus arisen. However, there is nothing wrong with good books of the past. All children need a knowledge of how our country came into being. Social history is more important than military or political.

Historical research is a fascinating pursuit. I did it for eight years myself. I was a research detective. I borrowed and read great stacks of books and took copious notes from them. I became adept in getting stories from other books. It was hard work, but fun too. I loved it. Until I made a mistake—the happy mistake of getting out of my book-lined studio . . . and going traveling . . . I made the mistake of seeing America for the first time, and the people who live in it and what they are doing . . . and I listened to them as they talked . . .

Now, please do not misquote me. Historical books, books which illuminate our past and tell of the people who lived before us, are a solid and important part of our literature, especially for children. Children need them and should not be without them.

I am just telling you how they are created.

An author may choose to escape into imagination. This can also be an evasion of real life.

There are children's writers who have no contact with children, who even dislike them in person (I have heard them say so) and yet they know what children like, and it is usually an imaginative story. Even those authors who do like children and enjoy their companionship are prone to get stories from their imagination. It has become a fetish, "the thing"—a story for a child should, of course, be imaginative.

In imaginative writing they try their wings, try cutting themselves loose from reality and exploring an infinite potential . . . They want no strings attached to plebian earth, no consideration of real life or people to enter in. Frankly, this is not possible. You cannot cut loose from the world of reality even if you think you can. For instance, try to create an imaginary animal. Try to imagine an animal that has never before existed. It just cannot be done. Even Dr. Seuss cannot do it. He just puts parts of other animals together in a different way. The human mind cannot invent something absolutely new, it cannot divorce itself from Mother Nature.

In escaping into imagination, we have gone a long way beyond pretty princesses, fairies and goblins and little elves and gnomes and wicked witches and dreadful stepmothers. Now we go to the moon and the orbiting planets. We consort with space-men and men from Mars, not to mention monsters and batman. We associate with rockets and missiles and satellites. We glory in science fiction, whether scientific or not. The important thing is that it must be cut off as far as possible from the real life of the present. Of such books, let us be generous and say: there are always harmless trends like this—they have their little day. Children like them for awhile and read them. Then they are gone and completely forgotten.

If creating out of the imagination means creating out of a vacuum, it gets nowhere. The author thinks up quaint conceits, cute ideas like putting a face on the engine of a train to personalize it. This is an adult's imagining—no child ever imagined a train going by itself.

Now there have been great books written out of the imagination, but imagination with one foot on the ground. I give due honor and respect to any modern author who can create a work of fantasy, fit to stand beside the great imaginative books of the past. Children love fantasy—not all the time, but now and then, and at certain stages of their development, and they should have books of fantasy. They should have fairies and goblins, if they want them. They should have fairy tales, *Wind in the Willows* and *Alice in Wonderland* and all the others, as part of a wholesome well-rounded book diet.

But I maintain that it is a difficult task for any modern author to compete with the old legendary folk and fairy tales, or with the works of fantasy written by the great authors of the past—Kenneth Grahame and James Barrie, Lewis Carroll and others. It is a difficult but not impossible task for a work of true imaginative integrity to spring forth from this present mechanistic industrialized day and age. If it can be done, more power to the valiant author who accomplishes it.

Even the world of the imagination should have its roots in the earth, in human beings. You cannot create out of a vacuum. You have to go to life, the source of all things. The world around us, the earth, the things that grow on it, the men who inhabit it, who make shelter and get food and clothing and fill their basic needs from the earth, is the source. The world and life itself is the basis for all ideas. Life itself is the book of all books.

There is a third way of escape—into artificial life, with so-called true-to-life books. Some authors try to write of real life but fail when their creating comes from WITHIN. Yes, they will write about people, the kind they hatch up in their brains, not those they see at the laundromat or the supermarket. They want to write about *nice* people, so in their books, people become puppets or cardboard dolls instead of flesh and blood.

Parents can do no wrong. They are often conveniently absent or off-stage, so children can accomplish fantastic adventures, the more far-fetched the better. Parents, if on stage, are always sweet and amiable. Daddy never drinks or swears or gets angry. He has an unspecified job with an unlimited salary, which provides an up-to-date house with a TV set and a telephone in every room and at least two cars in the garage. Mommy never soils her hands or scolds the children or yells at them. She never does any noticeable work and is always dressed in the latest style. Somehow, a lot of authors have succeeded in building up this cozy myth of adult perfection. The parents I have met in real life are not like this at all.

In such books, children themselves are paragons of virtue, affected little prigs, who love to work impossible miracles, and so we have hundreds of lifeless, bloodless, pretty-pretty Pollyanna stories.

This picture of artificial life in America has been buttressed and promoted by two other agencies. First, by the movies, which present a vivid picture of the life that real people do not live; and second, by the advertisers, who try to make readers believe that everybody in America lives the lives they picture with all the gadgets they advertise.

Sylvia Ashton-Warner, New Zealand teacher, when looking over a batch of American primers and textbooks, said: "Don't American children ever yell and scream? Don't they ever get angry? Don't they ever hate anybody and fight? Does it never rain or snow in America?" Judging from our textbooks, Miss Warner thinks the life of American children must be all perfection. Those who teach flesh-and-blood children daily, know this is far from true. But one could never guess it from the textbooks we give them to read, from our books of poetry and from the stories of artificial life which fill the bookshelves of our libraries.

We live in a changing world. It is changing so fast, it is making some of us dizzy. Those of us who lived in horse-and-buggy days often look back with nostalgia and look forward with fear and trepidation. Where are we heading? We have recently waked up to a new world of electronics and computers, of adding machines, (no need to learn how to add any more) and Xerox copying machines, (no need to take notes any more, just swipe what you want out of any book and have a copy made) and tape recorders to take away everybody's privacy. We've added a lot of new words to our vocabulary—the children have too. We talk glibly of automation, atomic energy, urban renewal, space travel—of missiles and rockets and jets and astronauts and launching pads and Lord knows what else. It's a bright new world all right and what the world of the future will be I hesitate to contemplate. I'm just thankful I won't be here!

Recently an important educator gave me some facts. He said that already only 6% of our population is still living on farms. Urbanization is increasing so fast that by 1975 95% of our children will be living in cities or suburbs. There won't be any rural areas left any more. Rural life is disappearing. City life is coming fast for all of us. The Atlantic coast will in a few years be a huge megalopolis from the tip end of Florida to the tip end of Maine. We have to get used to this new idea, for there are penalties we must pay.

Urban frustration is a new phrase lately being used. A major frustration will be the difficulty of transportation. Nobody will be able to get from one place to another. The biggest frustration will be alienation from nature. If all our children are living in the city in twenty years' time, they will know little or nothing of the world of nature first hand. They will never know the smell of a flower, never see a bluejay on the branch of a tree, never hold a butterfly in their hand. They will never wade a muddy stream, never go barefoot through the grass, never climb a tree—there will be no trees to climb—never romp with a dog down a country road. They will never feel the farmer's closeness to the elements or his dependence on the vagaries of the weather. The only landscape they will know is landscape in concrete. Where will their roots grow? In the cracks in the sidewalk?

We hope there will be a little park near by . . .

> *"Within the city of brick and stone,*
> *A square of green grows all alone.*
> *Green of trees and green of grass,*
> *With winding walks where people pass.*
> *Lake of water, boats to ride—*
> *Gentle waves from side to side.*
> *Do not pick the flowers gay,*
> *On the walks the children play.*
> *Sloping hills, green the grass,*
> *A pretty park where people pass."*

We hope the new freeways and high-rise apartments will not wipe out all the parks—with a little green grass.

There will be city life advantages—music and concerts and museums and art exhibits; and some aspects of nature cannot be taken away—the beauty of the sunshine, the wetness of the rain, contrasts of daylight and dark, of heat and cold, of wind and calm, of summer and winter. A sunset can still be beautiful behind a black silhouette of industrial smoke stacks. But even with these, there will be many lacks in the child's life.

Poetry has the great virtue of pointing out the truth in the fewest possible words, of seeing things with the fresh eager eyes of a child. What will a city child's life be like?

"The sidewalk is my yard,
The lamp post is my tree;
Up three long flights of stairs,
My home is Flat 4C.

The fire escape my porch,
Where clothes hang out to dry;
All day the noise and rush,
All night the trains go by.

Tall buildings all around
Reach up and shadow me;
Sometimes the great big sun
Comes peeping round to see.

All day the people pass,
They hurry as they go;
But when they are my friends,
They stop and say hello."

Yes, the city streets will be full of people. There will be people above, below and all sides. The one thing the city child will need to know most is how to get along with people.

Even in this fast-changing world, people are not, like the leopard, going to be able to change their spots. People are still going to be human beings with all their orneriness, contrariness and cantankerousness. People will still be able to quarrel and fight and gossip about each other, to settle their differences with their fists, and I think they will still be able to be kind and generous and to give a little love to each other. In spite of violence, crime and ruthlessness, there will still be a place in the world for beauty, tenderness and mercy.

In this bright new world of the future, children are still going to be able to laugh and cry, they are going to need their faces washed and their runny noses wiped, to be scolded and spanked and loved and petted. People are still going to eat, drink and sleep, maybe not work—just play all day, but they'll still be human beings. This will still be the universal human condition, so why not write about it? Even if we try to change human nature, we cannot. And yet, some authors say, "There's no drama in everyday life." No drama? Actually, there's nothing else but.

The eternal verities do not change.

Certain things are as true now as they were long ago in the tents in the desert in the days of Abraham, in the rice-fields of China, in the ghettoes of Europe, in the tepees of our American Indians. They are just as true as in this world of today and as they will continue to be in the new world of tomorrow.

We are all the same underneath. It is only the outward camouflage, the protective covering that is different, that changes. A mother is a mother. She is as good (or as bad) a mother, dressed in long trailing skirts with a gun on her shoulder, protecting her child from howling wolves in pioneer days, or dressed in tight-fitting shorts, with her hair in rollers under a net, pushing her child through a maze of city traffic in the present day. Motherhood and parenthood and childhood are the same the world over, in the world of the past or the present or the future.

"We are all the same—
Rich or poor
Young or old
Sick or well
Angry or calm
Happy or sad
Wise or foolish
Loving or hating
Hopeful or despairing—
We are all the same."

As for the children, to make up for the lacks

in their lives, books become more important than ever; a book has to become a *gift by proxy.* It has to give the child meaning in his own life, extension of his life experience into wider channels, beauty in the commonplace, the satisfaction of sharing the lives of others who suffer the same lacks or those with their lacks fulfilled. Teachers already know this. They have to be proxies. They have to provide a mother's love or supplement it, be a substitute mother, adding to the little or no love given by a real mother. A child who has no father can read in a book that others are fatherless too, or read of a father's warm love and so get vicarious experience.

A book will have to do so many things in this bright new world of the future. It will have to give the child nature by proxy, give him family security and love by proxy, help him feel the grass beneath his feet by proxy, while he walks the hard pavements of life. A book will be a gift by proxy to bring him a new grasp on reality. Children who have never seen a cow, who think milk is manufactured in the automatic coin-box milk machine on the sidewalk beside the high-rise apartment house will have to learn about cows from books.

Recently a girl in Baltimore wrote me: "We live in an apartment and can't have any pets, but I want a dog and a turtle, and my brother wants a cat and a fish. I also want a rose garden. Living in an apartment makes me feel closed up." A clear case of urban frustration. (I did not "make up" this child's letter, even though I am an enthusiattic gardener!)

But we must remember that children will always be children—in any country, in any age, in any environment. Right now, *Ring-a-round-a Rosie* is being played in China and India, Germany, France and England, over North and South America, in fact, all over the world. Boys are playing marbles in Japan and India and Greece and England. The game of marbles is as old as the stone age. Five busy plants in West Virginia, the world's marble center, are turning out ten million marbles a year. So let us take heart. "Batman" may come and "Batman" may go, but marbles go on forever!

In the slums of East Chicago, where children live in a distressing environment, I heard children chanting:

"Last night and the night before
Twenty-four robins came to my door

I came out and let them in,
They hit me on the head
with a rolling pin.
Lady, lady, turn around,
Lady, lady, touch the ground!
Lady, lady, show your shoe—
Lady, lady, is-ka-doo!"

Children make up their own jump-rope rhymes round the world—they do not read them in books. They hand them on to each other, changed and made timely in each generation.

All the mechanization and industrialization and scientific knowledge of the bright new world cannot kill out the human spirit. But child life must be fed, it must be nourished and not starved, and so we give it gifts by proxy to make up for all the lacks of its daily life. We must in person and through books give understanding, vicarious experience and beauty.

Books created from the OUTSIDE are books from life. Why should we write about the real life of today? Why put real people in books? Why put real incidents into books instead of imaginary ones?

For adults the great novels of the world have always dealt with human beings and their problems. Tolstoi and Dickens and Galsworthy and Faulkner and Hemingway and Maugham and many others wrote of real people. They found the lives of real people dramatic and tragic and lovable and well worth sharing with their readers. Why shouldn't children have the same? Because many authors are using their imaginations to orbit the earth and escape reality, it behooves some of us to stay down on earth and to give children grass-roots stories, to tell of real children and their stoicism, heroism, resilience and courage. To tell for instance, how twelve-year-old Darrell, with all the resourcefulness of a man, rounded up the herd of cows in a raging blizzard, on the prairies of South Dakota; how Felix adjusted to city life, although he was bitterly homesick for his old home in Alameda; how Joanda's little brother got his leg broken when the boss-man's tractor ran over it; how Dick gave up his dream of being a farmer because he loved animals so much; how Birdie Boyer helped with the strawberry crop and with her mother battled their malicious neighbors.

No drama in every day life? Who said that? Only a person blindfolded, egocentric and lacking in insight and discernment. No tragedy in a child's life? How about a penny lost in the grating of a city sidewalk, a pet dog run over by a car or a dead bird to be buried and a flower to be put on its grave? In the heart of the big city of Detroit, a mile from one of the biggest auto plants in the country, little Polish children enacted a touching funeral drama over a dead bird, for me. Little things, perhaps, to an obtuse adult, but real drama to a child. His own daily life is ever important for him to read about, to better understand himself and those around him.

Recently, a ten-year-old boy in Vermont wrote me: "I go to school just to hear my teacher read your books. Otherwise I'd stay home." Why? I wonder. There must be something in those books that touches his life and makes them meaningful.

How then can a writer claim that he knows real people and knows human nature well enough to write about real people. He cannot—the more I see of people, the more challenging and baffling they become. I make no claim of understanding them, only of trying to. All an author can do is to continue a never-ending study and search of motives, ideals, actions and happenings. But his very attitude of trying to learn, of never saying: I know it all, but remembering always how little he knows, picking up some sparks to light up his path, this attitude spurs him on his way. Projecting oneself into the life of another is difficult, if not frankly impossible. But this I must make clear, it cannot be done without the use of the imagination. Selectivity and imagination together convert actuality into the forms a story must take. My previous remarks regarding works of fantasy do not conflict with what I am saying now. No book, not even the simplest picture book, is created or comes into being without the use of the imagination. But the projection of oneself into the life of another is imagination of the highest order.

The ideal goal of a children's author should be to give children stories that have meaning in their daily lives, to give them poetry in words that they can understand on subjects that are close to them. To give them stories and poems that identify and give meaning to their life, that extend their life and make up for the lacks in their life. Simplicity, directness and meaning, these are the basic requirements.

My own books have come, not from within, but from without. They have come from two outside sources, from children and from the outside world of people and places. All that I know about children I have learned from children themselves, from observation, association and participation in their lives. All that I know about this country of ours and the contemporary life that people are living, I have learned from the people themselves and from a study of the environments in which they live. This knowledge, reflected in the stories, has enabled my readers to travel with me into the hearts and homes of others.

Dear Miss Lenski

DEAR CHILD

To you
who read my books
and write to me,
This poem will
my answer be.

All my books are stories true,
Of boys and girls and what they do.
Their lives may be strange,
Their customs new,
Yet underneath
They are much like you.
Outside different, inside akin,
Brothers and sisters under the skin.

To you
my love I send,
I am your friend,
A friend of children here and there,
A friend of children
everywhere.

HOW MANY LETTERS opening with these words have I had in the last forty years? The number cannot be counted. Sometimes they start, "Dear Lois," as if I were a close friend, the friend I hope to be to every child who reads my books.

Children not only inspire my books, help provide material for them, evaluate and criticize them, but keep me happy by writing enthusiastic fan letters. I try to answer them all—almost a thousand each school year—fearful that if I made a selection, I might neglect the very child to whom my letter would mean the most. One cannot always tell by the handwriting which letter is the most poignant, nor do the words themselves reveal the inarticulate message between the lines. I enjoy answering the letters, and I like to put a bookmark or folder into the envelope for an unexpected surprise.

No author can help wondering how her books are received by her public, whether children like and understand them, and whether the books are achieving the purpose she had in mind in writing them. It is a case of "casting bread upon the waters" and waiting for it to come back, as it does so richly and so often, over and over again, in tributes from both children and adults. Without fan letters, the direct response from one's audience, an author would be desolate indeed.

There are many kinds of fan letters. Some are stereotyped and lifeless; some are parrot-like, obviously echoing words the child is told to say. I can always detect the written-to-order letter. Some are of the book-report type: "Write of the most humorous incident; the most exciting part; the part you liked best; the saddest part, your favorite character—why?" Or: "Make a list of facts you learned from reading the story." Such letters are always lacking in spontaneity. I think the most monotonous letters I get are those that begin:

"The part I liked best was where Lolly fell in the bayou," or "where Billy had a fight with the neighbor boys."

Although the following letter from a Chinese boy in Honolulu is a recounting of facts, still it manages to convey the boy's enthusiasm:

> "I am reading *Cotton in My Sack* and enjoying it very much. It is very exciting. First Ricky had a broken leg, after that Lolly got burn, mother had heart attack, and the trailer of cotton got stole. And Joanda's library book got all muddy and she threw it in the stream. I wish you keep on writing book. They are wonderful."

Children's letters come filled with questions and certain basic ones are asked over and over:

> "Do you like to write books?
> When did you first start writing?
> What was the first book you wrote?
> How old were you when you wrote it?
> How long does it take to write a book?
> How many books have you written?
> Do you ever get tired of writing books?"

Some questions are biographical:

> "When and where were you born?
> Are you married? Have children? Ages?

Did you like to write when you were little?
What did you want to be when you were a child?
What books did you read as a child?
What book or books influenced your life?
What made you want to be a children's author?
How did you start your career?
How did it feel to get the Newbery medal?
Why do you write for children and not for adults?"

The use of the book, *Junior Book of Authors,* in the classroom would answer many of these questions and relieve the author of the responsibility. It would help the class to come to know many authors. My publishers have helped me by providing biographical sheets or booklets and folders to send out.

Some letters reveal a lack of guidance on the part of teacher or librarian.

When a child asks, "Is this book true? Did these things really happen?" it is easy to see that neither child nor teacher has read the foreword in the book. When the children ask, "Where do you get the ideas for your books? Do you make them up out of your imagination?" one can only conclude that the foreword has been skipped over, and my books have been put in the same class with other authors' imaginary tales. The whole purpose of my books—to widen the child's understanding by acquainting him with other American children and their ways of life, has been overlooked.

To such children, I reply: "You have missed the best part of the book. Go back now and read the foreword carefully. It will tell you how I got all my ideas from the real people I visited in the region itself." Once a child, writing for a fourth grade about *Judy's Journey*, said,"We liked it because it helped us in our study of Geography of the Atlantic States." My heart sank. It was most disheartening—the children had missed the real message of the book.

When a child says: "I liked the illustrations in this book. Who made the pictures?" it is obvious that he and his teacher have not even read the title page. Often children, although told of the authenticity of the book's background, still doubt it, perhaps because most of the books they read are entirely fictional or "made-up." To all the children who question the book's truth, a reading of the foreword would have set their minds at rest.

Even when children know that I write about real people and how I gather my stories, they often draw wrong conclusions. This shows the importance of wise guidance. Recently a reading consultant told me of his difficulty of getting a group of young teachers to realize the truth in my stories. He had to say to them: "Don't you know what the word *regional* means? These are truthful stories of actual regions!" "Oh!" was their astonished reply.

The child who wrote of *Strawberry Girl*: "We laughed and laughed at the funny way the people talked!" needs to be told that all people do not speak alike and that his own speech might sound equally "funny" and strange to a person from another part of the country; and that speech different from one's own is never a laughing matter. When children ask: "Why do you write about people like these?" I try to tell them of my love for all kinds of people, and of my desire to understand and know them, and to help children to understand and know them. Sometimes children do understand, perhaps feeling it instinctively. A boy wrote me, "I enjoy your books because they tell how much fun poor people can have." Many other examples can be cited, for despite indifference and lack of guidance, an author always has faith that the values in a book can reach the reader.

In contrast to the slight and disappointing

letters, there are others that are delightfully candid and amusing:

> "We acted out *Judy's Journey* today. We got out of Arithmetic at least."

> "I would like to write more but I can't think of anything to say because I am tired and have an awful headache."

> "I would like to ask you to send me your picture and some information about yourself for a book I am making. My teacher is pretty mean and we have to get our book in or get an E and I don't think I'd like that."

> "I liked *Texas Tomboy* because it's about a girl who didn't like school. I don't either. And she was always getting in trouble. So am I!"

But for delightful candor and outspokenness, this one is priceless:

> "Dear Miss Lenski: How are you? Have you wrote any more books for children? How come you did not write me back when I wrote to you? Didn't you get my letter? Since I wrote you, my mother had a baby. Do you have any boys or girls? If you have kids, how old are they? I like your books very much. I like the last book you wrote. *How many books have you wrote anyhow?*

How honest and refreshing children are! Two more letters bear this out. The first is a masterpiece of negatives:

> "I read your book *Strawberry Girl.* I thought it was very real and very unrealistic too. It was real because of the way you put real life-like characteristics to the characters. It was not real in the way that some of the things don't happen. I like the things that happen very much anyway. I like the way you wrote it especially and I don't think that if a different author wrote it, it would not be quite the same."

A little girl from Oklahoma, after seeing a snapshot of me standing in front of a large blooming lilac bush, wrote:

> "I shore wish you would tell me what kind of flowers you are standing by, because it is such a pretty one and you look very good too, standing by those lovely flowers if They give seeds I shore would like to have you send me some to put beside my dogs house."

What I look for always is a thoughtful evaluation from the child's own consciousness, and I have had many such letters. Reading my Regional books has often stirred young readers to tell me of their own lives in a frank and natural way, and this has in turn led to the choice of new regions to write about. Fan letters can be more than flattering words of praise to a favorite author. They can also be the means of establishing a friendly personal relationship with the author, and a feeling of confidence which leads to an actual sharing of the child's own life and of the group and the region, resulting in a new book.

When the children of Arkansas and South Dakota, and later those of Iowa and San Francisco, learned that I was writing honest stories based on children's actual experiences in real life in different parts of the United States, they wrote me saying:

> "Please come to our region and write about us. We are a part of America. We want to be in a book too."

I am deeply grateful for these children's letters, for without this concrete "lead" from the children themselves, these books would probably never have been written.

Many, many invitations come and keep coming which cannot be accepted. A girl in Wisconsin wrote recently:

> "Last night I had a dream and the dream was that

> you came to our school and stayed with the fifth grade class and wrote a book about us."

I was as disappointed as she that I could not make that dream come true. A boy from Ohio wrote poignantly:

> "I wish you would write a story about us. But I guess we're just people, knowbody special."

As an author reviews letters received over the years, there are many that are spontaneous, joyous and appreciative, concrete evidence that the real message has been conveyed. These letters come from the heart and are a great comfort.

Some letters reflect the intensity of the child's enjoyment:

> Your books are so interesting, I thought I was with the characters. I was reading *Prairie School* one afternoon when mother said, 'Charlotte, go get the clothes in.' I almost said, 'Do you want me to fall in a snowdrift?' You see I was at the part of the big snow."

> "I can't help calling you Lois, because you seem to know how a child my age, ten, thinks and feels. I would like it if you would write to me in your own handwriting."

> "I was reading *Judy's Journey.* The part I liked best was when Judy didn't go to a birthday party

because she didn't have a clean dress and no shoes and all the girls going to the party made fun of her."

"When I read your books, it's hard for me to quit. It seemed like everything was happening to me."

That children thus identify themselves with my book characters and feel the reality of the stories, there can be do doubt:

"The thing I like best about your books is that they are *so real to life*."

"We liked Joanda very much. She seemed like one of us."

"You get so you feel like you live in the same house as the characters in the story. Suzette is just like one of my friends now and I feel as if I had visited her, because I can see her house and her family so well."

"I really liked your book *Shoe-Fly Girl*. Sometimes you feel like you're the character in the book. You can laugh when they laugh and cry when they cry."

A copy of *Judy's Journey* found its way into the hands of a migrant boy:

"I saw one of your books and read it. The name of it was *Judy's Journey*. I liked that book because I lived almost the same way once. And I know how it feels to drink water out of canals, and sleep on the ground."

An Arkansas girl drew a picture of a house for *Judy's Journey*. She wrote beneath it:

"This is the place where they got them a home."

The main purpose of the Regional books (and of the Roundabout America books for younger children) in widening the child's horizon to greater understanding of others, is often reflected in the children's letters. The books arouse first awareness, then compassion. They take the child out of his own narrow life into the life of others:

"I just read *Prairie School*. It told all about the life in Dakota that I did not know about. I thought here in Iowa we had the worst blizzards. When our teacher read the book, I changed my mind about who had the worst blizzards."

"I like your book *Judy's Journey*. It helped me understand the meaning of a sharecropper. It also helped me to see just what a sharecropper has to do in order to make a living. I like Judy because she is a hard-working little girl.

"I have read *Cotton in My Sack*. I am very sorry to hear that it is true. I feel very sorry for this family when I read this book. We do not realize how lucky we are until we read a book like this. This family I think has went through a lot of sorrow."

"I took *Cotton in My Sack* home to read when school was out. I read it to my mother while she ironed. She liked it very much too. She used to live in Tennessee and she said it was so true to life. I thought Joanda was very nice. When I grow up I'm going to Arkansas to teach a school for sharecroppers, tenants and owners."

A fifth grade in Ohio wrote:

"Our teacher read *Judy's Journey* aloud to us and we did not want her to stop until it was finished. We are so interested in the children you write about, that we would *even like them to come to our school."*

Another fifth grade in Iowa said of *Strawberry Girl*:

"We liked this book. It taught us the lesson—to love our neighbor."

Some of my most rewarding tributes have come to me from mothers. Miriam S. Lind, a Mennonite mother, wrote me from Pennsylvania:

> "After reading your books, I can see developing in my children a marked compassion for and a loving acceptance of those 'beyond the rim of their own little world.' This compassion is not only a compassion for people in the story, but for people all around them. When my six-year-old son noticed that one little girl hid her lunch under the table so no one could see how poor it was, as they ate their warm cafeteria lunches, he wondered if we could not buy lunches for her, and not let her or any one know who was doing it. When our children call our attention to injustices and inequalities, when they stick up for a child who is being ridiculed by a group, when they fail to recognize any such things as class or race distinction, I feel that while our personal example has been good, the influence of good books has been of immeasurable help. I can only hope that this compassionate and loving regard of all people may be a growing spirit in them and that it will not suffer with the impact of an age which is in too big a hurry to be kind."

Just recently an Ohio mother, Mrs. E. Wollam, wrote, saying:

> "Among other influences in their lives, I believe your books played a significant role in developing a concern for others in our children's lives. For this we are grateful. Karen is a social worker, Gretchen a teacher, and Kristin plans to become a professional social worker on completing her university work."

Among my strongest supporters have been hundreds of teachers and librarians, who themselves believe in my books, and year after year, pass on their values to the children in their care. Many letters also come from students of children's literature or library science in colleges and universities, who are making special studies of my work from many different angles. All these tributes are heartening, but I think I love most those that come from children.

Some special few children go well beyond the call of duty in their letters, when the love for their "favorite author" turns into adoration. One can only hope to be worthy of such superlatives as these:

"Dear Lois Lenski:

I don't expect you to anser this. But I just wanted to tell you that I want to be a wrighter. You are my second favorit writer. My first is Lara Wilder. You must think I am silly and rude to put you in secont place. But if I was a wrighter I would feel vary proud out of all the books in the world mine was secont best! Lara Wilder is dead or so I have heard, so I feel that you have taken her place. And you should be rejoicing in God that your books have brought so much happiness to children all over the world."

Another ecstatic letter came also from California:

> "Dear Miss Lenski:
>
> You are the best author in the world. The reason I like you better than any author is because you write interesting books and once I start reading one of your books I can't get myself out of in when it's time to eat dinner. I am so interested in your books I can't let them go. Miss Lenski would you please send me a picture of you so I can hang it up in my room and look at it day and night?"

All fan letters, no matter how simple or how effusive, find a special place in an author's heart. They make me realize, as nothing else could, the rewards of writing for children.

E. O. PAINTER
PRINTING CO.
DE LAND, FLORIDA